THE
YEAR
IN REVIEW:
1991
People weekly
PRIVATE LIVES

The wedding party
(from top left)—Carole Bayer Sager,
Michael Jackson, bride Elizabeth Taylor,
groom Larry Fortensky, Norma Heyman,
Naomi Wilding; (from bottom left) Marianne
Williamson, Waldo Fernandez, Jose Eber, Mi-
chael Wilding Jr., Laela Wilding, Eliza Carson
(in headband), Christopher Wilding, Trip
Haenisch, Howard Taylor.

PRIVATE LIVES

THE YEAR IN REVIEW: 1991

COPYRIGHT 1992 THE TIME INC. MAGAZINE COMPANY

PUBLISHED BY OXMOOR HOUSE, INC.
BOOK DIVISION OF SOUTHERN PROGRESS CORPORATION
P.O. BOX 2463, BIRMINGHAM, ALABAMA 35201

PEOPLE WEEKLY is a registered trademark of
The Time Inc. Magazine Company

ISBN: 0-8487-1117-3
Library of Congress Catalog Card Number: 90-64375

Manufactured in The United States of America
First Printing 1991

PRIVATE LIVES
SENIOR EDITOR: Jane Kagan Vitiello
DESIGNER: Bob Cato
DIRECTOR OF PHOTOGRAPHY & RESEARCH: Geraldine Howard
PRODUCED FOR VITIELLO & CO. by Gregory Vitiello
RESEARCHER: Denise Lynch
COPY EDITOR: Patricia R. Kornberg

Special thanks to Jeremy Koch, Linda Rolle, Nancy
Lambert, Bob Briody, Mary Carroll Marden, Beth Filler,
Jereme Jones, Rachelle Naishtut, Candace Conard,
Kate Jennings, Roxanna Lonergan and Stacey Harmis.

COVER PHOTOGRAPH: Steve Schapiro

TO ORDER PEOPLE WEEKLY, write to:
PEOPLE WEEKLY
Subscription Service Department
P.O. Box 30603
Tampa, Florida 33630-0603

PRIVATE LIVES IS BASED ON THE EFFORTS OF THE EDITORIAL STAFF OF PEOPLE
WEEKLY.
MANAGING EDITOR Landon Y. Jones Jr.
EDITOR. SPECIAL PROJECTS Richard A. Burgheim
ASSISTANT MANAGING EDITORS Ross Drake, Cutler Durkee, John Saar.
Susan Toepfer. Carol Wallace, Hal Wingo
SENIOR EDITORS Lee Aitken, Mark V. Donovan. Dick Friedman. Jack Friedman.
Eric Levin. Ralph Novak. Joseph Poindexter, J.D. Reed. Roger R. Wolmuth.
Jacob Young
ART DIRECTOR John Shecut Jr.
PICTURE EDITOR Mary Carroll Marden
CHIEF OF REPORTERS Nancy Pierce Williamson
DEPUTY CHIEF OF CORRESPONDENTS Irene Kubota Neves
ASSOCIATE EDITORS Paula Chin, Daniel Chu. James S. Kunen.
Kristin McMurran, Jeannie Park. Leah Rozen. Maria Wilhelm
SENIOR WRITERS Ron Arias, Steven Dougherty, Mary H.J. Farrell.
Tom Gliatto, Michelle Green. David Grogan. Ken Gross. Bill Hewitt. David
Hiltbrand, Kim Hubbard. Bonnie Johnson, Michael J. Neill. William Plummer.
Susan K. Reed, Marjorie Rosen. Susan Schindehette, Karen S. Schneider.
Elizabeth Sporkin. Joyce Wadler

STAFF WRITERS Tim Allis. Peter Castro. Charles E. Cohen. Cynthia Sanz.
Joyce Wansley
WRITER-REPORTERS Toby Kahn, J.D. Podolsky. Lisa Russell
REPORTERS Peggy Brawley (Deputy Chief). Rosemary Alexander. Veronica
Burns. Maria Eftimiades. Ann Guerin, Mary S. Huzinec. Denise Lynch. Hugh
McCarten. Sabrina McFarland. Samuel Mead. Gavin Moses. Khoi Nguyen. Gail
Nussbaum. Vincent R. Peterson. Marge Runnion. Mary Shaughnessy. Ying
Sita. Maria Speidel. Leslie Strauss. Robin Ward
PICTURE DEPARTMENT Beth Filler (Deputy Editor). Holly Holden. Maddy
Miller (Associate Editors). Mary Fanette. Mary Ellen Lidon. Karen Lipton.
Sarah Rozen. Eileen Sweet. Anne Weintraub (Assistant Editors). Betsy Young
(Negative Reader). Blanche Williamson (Research). Stan J. Williams (Picture
Desk). Alison Sawyer. Karin Grant (Photo Chief. L.A.). Jerene Jones (London).
Francesca d'Andrea (Paris)
ART DEPARTMENT Hillie Pitzer (Deputy Director). Angela Alleyne (Assistant
Director). Mary M. Hauck (Designer). Tom Allison. Sal Argenziano. Allan
Bintliff. Scott A. Davis. Brien Foy. Joseph Randazzo. Ching-Yu Sun. Richard G.
Williams. Thelis Brown
COPY DESK Annabel Bentley (Chief). David Greisen. Will Becker. Marcia
Lawther (Deputies). Dolores Alexander. William Doares. Judith I. Fogarty. Ben
Harte. Rose Kaplan. Patricia R. Kornberg. Alan Levine. Eric S. Page. Mary C.
Radich. Muriel C. Rosenblum. Janet Scudder. Sheryl F. Stein (Copy Editors).
Deborah Hausler. Jessica Foos Jones. Lillian Nici. Patricia Rommeney (Assistants)
PRODUCTION Betsy B. Castillo. Geri Flanagan. David Luke. Gloria Neuscheler.
Paul Zelinski (Managers). Guy Arseneau. Catherine Barron. Kalen Donaldson.
Bernadette DeLuca. Patricia Fitzgerald. George Hill. Robin Kaplan. James M.
Lello. Maria Teresa Martin. Anthony G. Moore. Kathleen Seery. Warren
Thompson. Karen Wagner. Karen J. Waller. Anthony White
EDITORIAL TECHNOLOGY Amy Zimmerman (Director). Janie Greene.
Peter Klein
COPY PROCESSING Alan Anuskiewicz (Manager). Anthony M. Zarvos
(Deputy). Michael G. Aponte. Soheila Asayesh. Donna Cheng. Denise M.
Doran. Jayne Geissler. Charles J. Glasser Jr.. Nelida Granado. Key Martin.
Jennifer Paradis-Hagar. Barbara E. Scott. Ellee Shapiro. Larry Whiteford
PUBLIC AFFAIRS Beth Kseniak (Director). Jodi Mastronardi (Assistant Manager)
EDITORIAL BUSINESS MANAGER Sarah Brody. Maria Tucci (Deputy)
ADMINISTRATION Susan Baldwin. Bernard Acquaye. Marge Dodson. Angela
Drexel. Nancy Eils. Joy Fordyce. Deirdre Gallagher. Diane Kelley. Mercedes R.
Mitchell. Margaret Pienczykowski. Jean Reynolds, Pauline Shipman. Michael
Tanner. Martha White. Maureen S. Fulton (Letters/Syndication Manager)
NEWS BUREAU William Brzozowski. Charles Guardino. Dorothy Poole
NATIONAL CORRESPONDENT Lois Armstrong
DOMESTIC BUREAUS CHICAGO. Giovanna Breu. Barbara Kleban Mills.
Champ Clark; DETROIT. Julie Greenwalt; HOUSTON. Kent Demaret. Anne
Maier; LOS ANGELES. Jack Kelley. Michael Alexander. Lorenzo Benet.
Thomas Cunneff. Todd Gold. Kristina Johnson. Robin Micheli. Craig Tomashoff.
Florence Nishida. Monica Rizzo; MIAMI. Meg Grant; NEW YORK. Victoria
Balfour. Sue Carswell, David Hutchings; SAN FRANCISCO. Dirk Mathison;
WASHINGTON. Garry Clifford. Luchina Fisher. Linda Kramer. Jane Sims
Podesta. Margie Bonnett Sellinger. Barbara Lieber
EUROPEAN BUREAUS Fred Hauptfuhrer (Chief). Laura Sanderson Healy.
Terry Smith (London); Cathy Nolan (Paris)
SPECIAL CORRESPONDENTS ATLANTA. Gail Wescott; BOSTON. S. Avery
Brown; CHICAGO. Bonnie Bell. Civia Tamarkin; CLEVELAND. Ken Myers;
DENVER. Vickie Bane; INDIANAPOLIS. Bill Shaw; LOS ANGELES. Andrew
Abrahams. Doris Bacon. Mitchell Fink. Nancy Matsumoto. Vicki Sheff;
MEMPHIS/NASHVILLE. Jane Sanderson; MIAMI. Cindy Dampier. Linda
Marx. Don Sider; MINNEAPOLIS. Margaret Nelson; MONACO. Joel Stratte-
McClure; NEW ORLEANS. Ron Ridenhour; PARIS. Harriet Shapiro;
PHILADELPHIA. Andrea Fine; PITTSBURGH. Jane Beckwith; PORTLAND.
Susan Hauser; ROME. Logan Bentley; SAN DIEGO. A.F. Gonzalez;
SAN FRANCISCO. Dianna Waggoner; TEL AVIV. Mira Avrech; WASHINGTON.
Marilyn Balamaci. Katy Kelly
CONTRIBUTING PHOTOGRAPHERS Marianne Barcellona. Harry Benson.
Ian Cook. Tony Costa. Mimi Cotter. Alfred Eisenstaedt. Stephen Ellison.
Evelyn Floret. Henry Grossman. Kevin Horan. Steve Kagan. Christopher Little.
Jim McHugh. Robin Platzer. Neal Preston. Co Rentmeester. Raeanne Rubenstein.
Steve Schapiro. Mark Sennet. Peter Serling. Terry Smith. Barry Staver. Stanley
Tretick. Dale Wittner. Taro Yamasaki
EDITORIAL SERVICES Christiana Walford (Director). Jennie Chien. Benjamin
Lightman. Hanns Kohl. Beth Bencini Zarcone

CONTENTS

INTRODUCTION / 6

1991 . . . IN THE LIMELIGHT / 8

PRIVATE LIVES / 26

CRIMES & MISDEMEANORS / 36

PROVOCATIONS / 64

PROFILES IN COURAGE / 70

POSTSCRIPTS / 86

GOODBYES / 92

PHOTO CREDITS / 112

INTRODUCTION

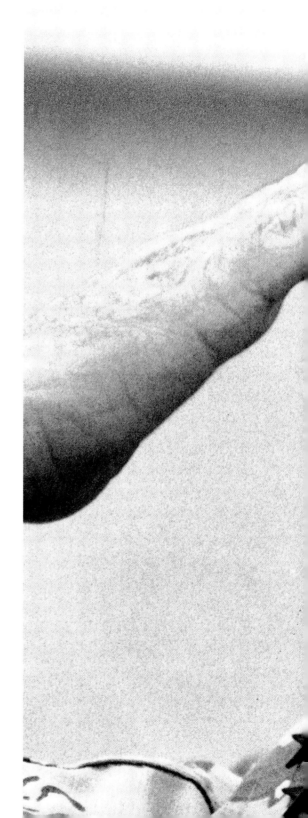

Welcome to the second annual edition of PRIVATE LIVES, a hardcover keepsake of yet another turbulent, triumphant and memorable year—1991. As we culled the weekly magazine for compelling pieces to preserve and update—and sought out fresh photographs to illustrate them—we found ourselves once again laughing, shaking our heads or feeling a lump in our throats. Undoubtedly, the most affecting chapter of the book is "Goodbyes," a tribute to figures who died during the year. Who among us will forget Michael Landon or Martha Graham or the fallen heroes of Operation Desert Storm? Our staff's ultimate feeling—and we trust it will be yours—was of compassion and hope for the human condition. We would like to believe that the subjects of the comeuppance items in this year's book will be the heartening comeback stories of next year's Volume III.

The Editors of PEOPLE

ELIZABETH TAYLOR

First things first. No, Bubbles did not carry the rings down the aisle. In fact neither Michael Jackson's beloved chimp nor his giraffe (also rumored to be in the wedding party) were anywhere to be seen on October 6, when Elizabeth Taylor Hilton Wilding Todd Fisher Burton Burton Warner, 59, winner of two Academy Awards, owner of the Krupp diamond and the living emblem of Hollywood glamour, married Larry Fortensky, 39, construction-equipment operator, at a lavish private wedding held on the grounds of Jackson's 2,700-acre estate near Santa Barbara, California.

Something like a dozen press-hired helicopters hovered overhead, dodging tethered hot-air balloons—meant to fend them off—as self-help guru and nondenominational minister Marianne Williamson made her way to a wooden gazebo for the ceremony. She was followed by Fortensky and his best man, hairdresser Jose Eber. Liz, deeply bronzed and exquisite in a pale-yellow, floor-length Valentino dress, was escorted by Jackson and her 38-year-old son, actor Michael Wilding Jr.

The helicopters drowned out the ceremony and caused more than a little alarm among the 160 guests seated directly below them. One intrepid tabloid photographer actually managed to parachute within 20 feet of the gazebo. Guards from the 100-man security force directed by Moshe Alon (a former Israeli army officer) made short work of the intruder's chute and quickly led him off. Taylor and Fortensky ignored all distractions as they pledged, "From this day forward you shall not walk alone. My heart will be your shelter, and my arms will be your home." The twice-divorced Teamster has been steadfastly devoted to Taylor since they met at the Betty Ford Center in 1988, where both were battling drug dependencies. The pair have been virtually inseparable since they emerged from rehab in late 1988.

As dusk fell, the bride and groom moved down a tree-lined candlelit walkway to the ivory, silk-draped reception tent provided by Jackson. (A perfectionist always, he'd had his gardeners dig up all his colorful flower beds and plant only white blooms.) Taylor took Fortensky's hand for the first dance, during which Michael Jackson and his date, Brooke Shields, cut in. Afterward, Taylor raised a glass of mineral water to her host, who reportedly picked up much of the estimated $1.5 million tab. "You've been so generous, it makes me want to cry," she said. "I'll never forget it as long as I live."

At about 10:30 P.M., the newlyweds sauntered off to Jackson's ranch house, where they spent several nights before a scheduled two-day tour to promote Taylor's new White Diamonds perfume.

Can a woman whose previous husbands have included some of the world's most affluent and powerful men find happiness with a working man who operates an off-road Caterpillar dirt compactor? Liz thinks so. "No boy is poor," she once said, "if he's rich at heart." □

JULIA ROBERTS It was going to be the fantasy wedding of the decade—the showbiz merger of Hollywood's most bankable star, Roberts, 23, and her mercurial actor-beau of more than a year, Kiefer Sutherland, 24. Just three days before they were to become man and wife on a 20th Century Fox soundstage, the two unceremoniously called the whole thing off.

"It has been mutually agreed upon that the wedding has been postponed," announced the stars' publicists jointly.

They fell for each other on the set of *Flatliners* in 1990, when Sutherland was still married to his first wife, actress Camelia Kath, 37, mother of his daughter, Sarah, 3. (He and Kath were divorced in early 1990.) Sutherland eventually moved into Roberts's million-dollar house in Los Angeles, and in March she began wearing a costly diamond ring.

Friday, June 14, the day the wedding was to have taken place, the would-be groom moved out of Julia's Hollywood Hills house. She was at the trendy Nowhere Café with actor Jason Patric, 24. Patric is the son of actor-playwright Jason Miller and the grandson of comic Jackie Gleason (Gleason's daughter Linda is his mother). He and Julia dated in her pre-Kiefer days. Later that day, Julia and Jason caught a commercial flight to London, then jetted to Dublin where they chastely booked separate rooms at the Shelbourne Hotel.

Roberts's breakup with Sutherland may have caught Hollywood by surprise, but there were early warning signs that the romance was in trouble. Last February

Kiefer briefly moved out of Julia's home and checked into the scruffy, $105-a-week St. Francis Hotel across the street from Hollywood Billiards Parlor, a favored hangout. He was seen several times in the company of Amanda Rice, a go-go dancer who performs under the name of Raven at the Crazy Girls Club in Hollywood and sometimes hangs out at the pool hall.

Sutherland returned to Julia's digs in mid-February. Three months later Rice tattled to a tabloid. She quoted Kiefer as saying that Julia was insecure about her looks, overly possessive and, since *Pretty Woman*, had turned into an "ice princess."

Kiefer's publicist, Annette Wolf, said emphatically that her client and Rice had never had an affair. Added a friend of Kiefer's: "He is extremely upset about this thing with Rice. There was nothing sexual." (When interviewed, the assistant manager of the Crazy Girls Club, Marwan Khalaf, said that Rice was on leave for breast augmentation.)

Just before the wedding, Julia headed for the chic Canyon Ranch Spa in Tucson with some friends. (She'd attended an elaborate wedding shower thrown for her, and Kiefer had already taken off for his 300-acre spread in Whitefish, Montana, to spruce things up for their planned honeymoon.) But who should turn up at the Canyon Ranch Spa the same weekend as Julia? None other than Jason Patric. No sooner had Julia returned to Los Angeles than the story broke that the wedding was off.

For Roberts, the breakup was not without precedent. She has a history of becoming involved with her leading men. Roberts lived with *Satisfaction* costar Liam Neeson, 38, when she was 19, and broke off an engagement to her *Steel Magnolias* screen husband, Dylan McDermott, 29, after meeting Kiefer on the set of *Flatliners* in 1990.

A source describes Julia as "practically living with Jason now." Yes, but for how long? □

JOHN TRAVOLTA

They said it would never happen, and they were very nearly right. Since John Travolta presented Kelly Preston with a six-carat engagement ring at the stroke of midnight last New Year's Eve in Gstaad, there has been at least one set of canceled wedding plans. But finally, one midnight in September, John, who is 37, and Kelly, who is 28, were married in a flower-filled salon of the Crillon Hotel in Paris. The ceremony was presided over by a French Scientologist minister (both bride and groom are avowed practitioners).

Before Travolta met Preston in 1988 while they were filming *The Experts*, his major affair had been with the late actress Diana Hyland. He was 23, Hyland was 41. She died in his arms in 1977, a victim of cancer. Rumors have linked Travolta with Olivia Newton-John when they were partnered in *Grease* and with Debra Winger after they costarred in *Urban Cowboy*. In the early '80s he was spotted with Brooke Shields. In May 1990 the *National Enquirer* made much of an alleged liaison with male porn star Paul Barresi, who claimed that Travolta had picked him up in a health-club shower room in 1982. Barresi, who had a small part in Travolta's flop *Perfect* in 1985, said their affair—which is denied by Travolta's publicist—ended early that year.

Preston, divorced from actor Kevin Gage (her costar in *SpaceCamp*) after a two-year marriage, became engaged in 1989 to actor Charlie Sheen. When their relationship ended, they sold the 2.5-carat, $200,000 ring he had given her and split the proceeds.

The Travolta wedding was attended by just four of the couple's intimate friends and associates. Apparently the marriage was not registered with French authorities, raising questions about its legality. But at a press conference Travolta insisted that the pair would wed again in a U.S. civil ceremony "when we get over our jet lag." And, presumably, before the birth of the baby they expect in the spring. □

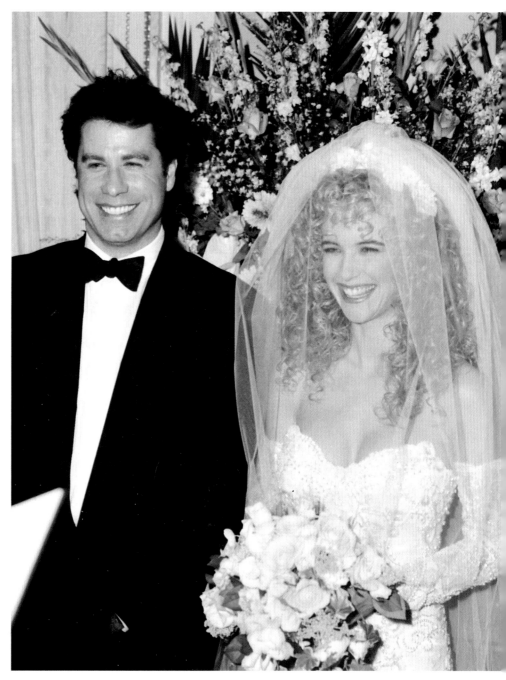

HARRY HAMLIN On a Saturday in September, at a picturesque Carmel Valley estate they had rented, *L.A. Law*'s Harry Hamlin, 39, married *Knots Landing*'s Nicollette Sheridan, 26. The Episcopalian ceremony was marred only by the clatter of helicopters overhead and prenuptial buzz about tabloid photos of Hamlin, in his underwear, ogling a stripper at his bachelor party.

The Hamlins' affaire de coeur began shortly after their first encounter in the fall of 1989, during preproduction for the Showtime movie *Deceptions*. "I could sense something was going to happen between them," recalls producer Ruben Preuss. "They talked about cars. She had a white Porsche and he had a black one." (Before they could ride off into the sunset, though, Hamlin first had a nasty divorce battle with his wife of four years, former *Falcon Crest* star Laura Johnson.) Harry carried a pear-shaped diamond engagement ring with him "for months, waiting for the right time to pop the question," he confides, before he finally did—on both knees, atop an undisclosed mountain.

After she said yes, the couple's search for a fitting wedding site ended when Nicollette's mother suggested the elegant country estate Stonepine in Carmel Valley. "We wanted a location that was synonymous with who we were," says Harry. "A place that was elegant but rustic and not pretentious at all."

Some three months of intensive planning later, the couple exchanged traditional vows before 200 guests. Not present was Hamlin's son by his longtime lover, 54-year-old Swiss-born actress Ursula Andress. Eleven-year-old Dmitri forsook the role of ring bearer to get back to school in Italy. "I tried to talk him into staying," says the bride. "He knows that he was wanted."

For all the glamour, the newlyweds admit there were a couple of hitches. "When the minister gathered the ushers," says Hamlin, "this huge industrial helicopter came swooping down over the site. An 18-piece symphony orchestra was playing the processional music and you couldn't hear it."

"It's amazing to me that the paparazzi could take such a beautiful, spiritual ceremony and obliterate it," says Sheridan. "If I'd had a rifle, I would have shot 'em down."

"The choppers were hovering above us," says Hamlin, but when his bride arrived for the ceremony in an open horse-drawn carriage, "I forgot about them completely. She walked up the aisle and, I mean, I was transported to another realm. I was not there. I was on a spiritual plane with Nicollette." □

WARREN BEATTY

In February, he squired 22-year-old model Stephanie Seymour to a 50th birthday party for Tri-Star Pictures head Mike Medavoy. Two months later, arriving alone at agent Swifty Lazar's post-Oscar party, he discovered ex-squeeze Madonna, fresh from her onstage performance vamping, grinding and patting herself. The Material Girl had shown up at Spago with Michael Jackson, but it was Beatty who took over the fondling chores.

That was then. This summer, the legendary romantic rover and actress Annette Bening, 33, who costars in Beatty's film, *Bugsy*, announced they were expecting a baby.

"We are happy to confirm that we are looking forward to the birth of a child early next year," the couple said in a statement from Beatty's publicist. Later, in response to a phone call, Beatty faxed a handwritten note to PEOPLE. "As you might have guessed, I'm still avoiding talking to the press about personal things," he wrote, "but I can tell you I couldn't be happier about having a baby with Annette."

The two got the news in mid-July. Bening, who was to have played Catwoman in the Batman sequel, phoned director Tim Burton and dropped out. Fearing her hasty exit would spark rumors, the couple chose to go public.

For the 54-year-old Beatty, this had been one of the more discreet relationships in his three decades of on-set entanglements. In 1961, his affair with *Splendor in the Grass* costar Natalie Wood helped sink her first marriage to Robert Wagner. Later, Beatty romanced Julie Christie (*McCabe & Mrs. Miller*), Isabelle Adjani (*Ishtar*) and, of course, Madonna (*Dick Tracy*)—to name but a few.

Bening, a Kansas-born actress who received an Oscar nomination for *The Grifters*, had been dating Ed Begley Jr. prior to meeting Beatty at a *Bugsy* rehearsal last January. She initially dismissed the notion that they would become involved. (Her resolution was apparently short-lived.)

Even so, nobody anticipated parenthood —except, presumably, the couple themselves. "There are no accidents in Warren's life," says his publicist, Andrea Jaffe. "If he didn't want to have a baby, he wouldn't have one." The blessed event will induct him into an emerging 50-plus paternity fraternity that now includes Dennis Hopper, Al Pacino and old friend Jack Nicholson.

For Beatty, one of the attractions of Bening—who is divorced from director J. Steven White—may be that she is as private as he is, or more so; it was Warren who had to persuade *her* to go public. "You don't understand," he told her. "It *is* a big deal." ☐

MARIAH CAREY

Three years ago Mariah Carey was sleeping on the floor of a shared apartment. Now she's pop's top-ranking rookie diva, with three hits and two Grammys—for Best New Artist and Female Pop Vocalist—to her credit.

Carey claims she has known what she wanted to be since she was 4 years old. By then she was already taking vocal lessons from mother Patricia, a onetime singer with the New York City Opera. Mom, of Irish ancestry, and Carey's dad, an engineer whose bloodlines are African-American and Venezuelan, had divorced a year earlier. For the next 15 years, Carey moved often as her mother looked for work as a singing coach. At 18, armed with a five-octave range of her own, Carey set out to pursue a music career.

For 10 months she waitressed and haunted New York City recording studios before winning an audition as a backup vocalist for R&B's Brenda K. Starr. "Most singers," says Carey, "would have said, 'Stay in the background and don't sing too loud.'" Instead Starr helped Carey land a record contract leading to her debut album in June 1990.

Carey demurs when critics compare her to Whitney Huston ("I've written all my songs; Whitney is not a writer"). Worse was one critic noting that she "is being marketed as the white Whitney Huston." Carey considers herself a "multicultural, interracial person who'll only make a point of it if I choose to, when people are misrepresenting or misinterpreting me." ☐

ROSEANNE BARR ARNOLD

When Roseanne Barr and Tom Arnold married in a civil ceremony a year ago, Barr told Arnold she would change her name to his if—and when—he converted to Judaism. On June 23 they celebrated 17 months of marriage and Tom's conversion with a second wedding at a Los Angeles synagogue. Afterward the couple and some 500 guests danced to "Kung Fu Fighting."

It was a Roseanne-esque choice. From singing the national anthem off-key to mud-wrestling with her Tom in a *Vanity Fair* photo spread, TV's most outspoken comedienne has seldom shunned notice or controversy. In the past, whatever the result of her antics, her intent was always to be funny. That changed dramatically in October when she stood before an audience of 1,000 adult incest survivors and therapists at Montview Boulevard Presbyterian Church in Denver and said, "My name is Roseanne and I am an incest survivor."

Roseanne says that she was sexually abused during her childhood but had suppressed the memories until a triggering incident nearly two years ago caused them to come flooding back. She, her three children and husband Tom have since undergone intensive therapy.

Roseanne's parents, Helen and Jerome Barr, have categorically and vehemently denied their daughter's allegations. Responded Roseanne: "They have told all their friends and all of our extended family that I am 'crazy old Roseanne,' striking out at them again for no reason. But this time, Mom and Dad, this time it just won't work." □

GERARDO

A bandanna partially covers his long, jet-black hair. The leather jacket, with the words LATIN TILL I DIE on the back, is open to expose a shirtless torso; tight blue jeans hang suggestively low in front. His sexy bilingual single, "Rico Suave," is No. 7 on *Billboard*'s pop charts. The song's hypnotic video, an MTV favorite, features gyrating Gerardo Mejia—known to his fans simply as Gerardo—stroking the legs of women and mouthing lyrics like "We'll be back early/Five, six, or seven in the morning/Your daughter is in good hands." The chorus, "rico, suave"—which Gerardo translates as "smooth and tasty"—is delivered in a rich, insinuating Spanish accent.

The 26-year-old native Ecuadoran was born in Guayaquil and moved with his family to California in 1976. Gerardo says he was just a typical suburban kid until the summer before his senior year. "Then I got wild," he says. "It all started happening, the women and stuff." Still, Gerardo managed to graduate and planned on becoming an accountant like his father, until he started winning dance contests at local clubs.

A small part as a tough motorcyclist in *Winners Take All*, a 1987 movie, was followed by a role as a football player in the teen flick *Can't Buy Me Love*, with Patrick Dempsey. That led to the bigger role of Bird, the gang member who kills Robert Duvall in Dennis Hopper's 1988 movie, *Colors*. Offscreen, Gerardo sang for a while with a reggae band but soon returned to Spanish-influenced rap. His album, *Mo' Ritmo* (*ritmo* means rhythm), was released last January.

Gerardo's aversion to shirts, he insists, is not a Hollywood put-on but a matter of being true to himself. "That's my look," he insists. Nevertheless, he does throw on a tank top for dinner, "out of respect for my parents." □

BRUCE SPRINGSTEEN

For Bruce Springsteen, the once-scruffy bar-band leader turned rock Boss, and his tambourine-whacking backup singer, Patti Scialfa, it was a traditional June nuptials. The setting, in the garden of the $14 million Beverly Hills estate that Springsteen, 41, and Scialfa, 37, have shared since last year, was worlds away from the New Jersey back streets where the singer and the Boss first met.

The bride, who had never been married before, wore a floor-length white gown decorated with pearl teardrops. The groom wore a classic black tuxedo, as he did at his 1985 wedding to actress-model Julianne Phillips, who divorced the Boss in 1989, after his much-publicized affair with Scialfa during their 1988 Tunnel of Love tour. Friends claim Springsteen and Phillips had nothing in common. In addition to similar backgrounds, the big bond between the Boss and Scialfa is Evan James, their 11-month-old son.

The couple exchanged rings and vows—composed by themselves, naturally—in a moving candlelight ceremony. □

DELTA BURKE On an

early summer day, Delta Burke, 34, late of the CBS sitcom *Designing Women,* and her husband of two years, Gerald McRaney, 43, the star of another CBS sitcom, *Major Dad,* renewed their wedding vows at a plantation outside New Orleans. Dixie Carter, Burke's costar and matron of honor in the previous ceremony in Los Angeles, was not in attendance. Neither were any of the other principals connected with *Designing Women.* Just eight days before her second wedding ceremony, the tempestuous Burke had been informed that Columbia Pictures Television was not renewing her $55,000-per-episode contract.

For five seasons *Designing Women* chronicled the antics at the Atlanta interior-decor firm of Sugarbakers. The show was popular and so was Burke, as zany, zaftig Suzanne Sugarbaker. Backstage, however, a feud simmered.

Some on *Designing Women* believe that what Burke really wanted was to be the series' star. Producers Harry Thomason and his wife, Linda Bloodworth-Thomason, were determined to maintain an ensemble of equals. Burke's agent claims his client never asked for star status. Whatever. Burke griped in her hometown newspaper, the *Orlando Sentinel*, that the set was "not a good workplace, not a good environment." The Thomasons countered with: "We are all mentally exhausted from the daily trials and tribulations of Delta Burke."

Sources on *Designing Women* believe that Delta's marriage to McRaney did not help the situation. She has said, "He wanted me to speak up and not take this treatment a long time ago." Burke met the twice-divorced McRaney when he made a 1987 guest appearance on the show, playing one of Suzanne's ex-husbands. Until then, the actress, who says she was molested at age 4, was afraid of men and rarely dated.

Eventually Burke's problems came to dominate the set. These included a notoriously fiery temperament, what costar Jean Smart described as "a childlike quality," and Burke's ongoing struggle with her weight—the 5′5″ former beauty queen once reportedly ballooned as high as 210 lbs. (The weight gain inspired her Emmy-nominated 1990 episode, "They Shoot Fat Women, Don't They?") In the end, many disgruntled colleagues, weary of what they saw as her mercurial nature and husband McRaney's off-the-set interference ("He's the force behind the mouth," said one), wished her good riddance.

Strangely enough for a controversy so public, Burke's fate may have been sealed by a private poll. Though the actress had requested a release from her contract late in 1990, that request was widely considered a negotiating ploy. But the following March, at a spontaneous, informal meeting (Burke had already left the set after filming her segments), the cast and producers voted on whether she should return to the show. The verdict was no. Burke got the news of her departure not from a production-company representative but by overhearing a conversation on the set of a CBS TV movie she and McRaney were filming.

The sixth season of *Designing Women* began with some cast replacements: Julia Duffy, formerly of ABC's *Baby Talk*, and Jan Hooks from NBC's *Saturday Night Live*. Burke emerged with a deal for a new, as-yet unwritten sitcom at Universal Television.

"Thanks for hiring me," Burke wrote the Thomasons. "Thanks for letting me go. It's the in-between part that we had problems with." □

BLACK POWER

Twenty years ago, with the release of his X-rated *Sweet Sweetback's Baadasssss Song*, Melvin Van Peebles, now 58, became the godfather of modern black cinema. But when the Chicago-reared Van Peebles first arrived in Hollywood in 1958, he showed his three short reels to every studio in town and was quickly disabused of his dream. "I'd tell them I wanted to be in film, thinking I could start in the editing room or as a production assistant," he says. "They'd say, 'How nice'—and offer me a job as an elevator operator."

For Hollywood's black community, the Van Peebles story is both a glimpse of history and a sign of the times—times that are getting better. This year alone, blacks have directed 19 films—more than were released all through the '80s. Melvin's own son, Mario, 34, made his film directorial debut with *New Jack City*, a black gangster flick that cost only $8.5 million to make and has brought in more than $68 million at the box office. "History," says Melvin, "has vindicated me." Hip to the times, studios are snapping up young directors off inner-city streets like Matty Rich, 19—and fresh out of film school—and like USC grad

John Singleton, 23. Says Spike Lee: "I don't think there has ever been a better time than now to be a young African-American filmmaker."

But along with success have come unforeseen problems. *Boyz N the Hood*, Singleton's semiautobiographical coming-of-age tale set in the embattled turf of his own south central Los Angeles, opened to critical acclaim—and gang-related gunfire. Some insist that films like *Boyz* and *New Jack City*, whose opening was marred by similar outbreaks, are incendiary. But film critic Roger Ebert disagreed. "*Boyz* makes a powerful statement against exactly the kind of street violence that is being associated with it," he wrote. "Nothing on the screen could have possibly inspired any trouble—just the reverse."

Though at least eight theaters canceled plans to show *Boyz*, most refused to change their marquees. "I'm not prepared to give up," said Alan Friedberg, chairman of Loews Theatres, which has 878 movie houses in 16 states. "I'm not prepared to cooperate in the killing of an idea." Or the killing of a profit. Showbiz, it is said, is neither black nor white but green. And while Hollywood (whose audience is 25 percent black) continues to cash in on its black talent—*Boyz* cost $6 million to make and took in $10 million-plus its debut weekend—the African-American moviemaking community is cashing in on its newfound cachet. Says Warrington Hudlin, producer of 1990's successful *House Party* and head of the Black Filmmaker Foundation: "For the first time, the authorship and control of the creative strings are ours."

Team spirit abounds among Hollywood's newly empowered blacks, but make no mistake: Every player has a different take on how to win. Are street-smart directors from the projects more authentically "black" than their college-

educated colleagues, as has suggested Matty Rich—who hails from Brooklyn's Red Hook section and made *Straight out of Brooklyn*? No, snaps third-generation Morehouse College graduate Spike Lee: "It's that kind of ignorant thinking that has black kids failing on purpose in class because they're ostracized for getting good grades or speaking good English." Okay then, should black producers hire predominantly black staff and crew, as Lee contends? No way, objects rapper and *New Jack City* star Ice-T. "That's a reverse racism thing." The perspectives are endless. As Mario Van Peebles puts it, "We are *not* one monolithic force." Says Brett King, director of television development for Quincy Jones Entertainment: "It's not that we want to see the black point of view, we want to see *a* black point of view."

Groupthink that categorizes black professionals by color rather than by ability and measures their work by the same stunted yardstick is deeply frustrating to many Hollywood blacks. "When I go to see a Martin Scorsese film, I don't say, 'Oh, what a wonderful white Italian film.' I say, 'Jesus, what a great film,'" says director Bill Duke, whose *A Rage in Harlem* opened this year.

In the end, blacks will have to build and hold their own power. "Progress has got to come from black companies and black directors," says Quincy Jones, whose own multimillion-dollar Quincy Jones Entertainment—which produced *Thriller* and *The Color Purple*—is perhaps the most important black media conglomerate this side of Motown. Jones, like his black colleagues, wants to settle—and rewrite—the Hollywood score. "I've been preparing for this for 40 years. So far, we're just making a dent," he says. "But we intend to blow your mind." □

Back row, from left: Warrington Hudlin, Reginald Hudlin, Ernest Dickerson, Mario Van Peebles. Center row: Spike Lee, Matty Rich, John Singleton. Front: Charles Lane.

RANDY TRAVIS After years of denying they were a duo, country superstar Randy Travis and his manager and housemate of 15 years, Lib Hatcher, have finally gone public—and legal. Last May, attended by two strangers brought by the preacher, the couple were married in the courtyard of one of their two Maui homes.

Some may find the romance hard to believe because Travis, 32, and Hatcher, 48, labored for so long to hide it. "It seemed easier than to explain everything to every interviewer you talked to," says Travis. Hatcher worried that the relationship would hurt Travis's career. "He was young, and you want to attract that young audience," she says. "I wanted him to appear available."

Then, last March, a supermarket tabloid ran a story implying that the two-time Grammy winner was gay. Angrily denying the suggestion, Travis started talking at last and told the *Washington Post* that he and Hatcher had been involved for 12 years.

A native of Kernersville, North Carolina, Mary Elizabeth Hatcher met Randy Traywick in 1977 when the 17-year-old came into her Charlotte, North Carolina, nightclub to audition for the weekly talent competition. The second of six children, Traywick (Travis is a stage name) had grown up in Marshville, North Carolina. His father encouraged his four sons to be country singers. By the time Randy was 10, his voice was already attracting attention at local dances and lodges; soon his behavior began attracting the attention of the police. "I got into a lot of trouble, drinking and taking drugs by the time I was 12," he admits.

When he walked into Hatcher's club, he had already been jailed several times for drunk driving and was facing a five-year prison stretch for breaking into a convenience store. Hatcher persuaded the judge to release him into her custody and brought him home to live with her and Frank, her husband of 10 years. Travis sang and washed dishes at the club to earn his keep. But when Frank told Lib to choose between their marriage and Randy, Hatcher and Travis moved out. "I never spoke to the man again," she says.

In 1986, after Travis's first album, *Storms of Life*, spawned five No. 1 singles, the ninth-grade dropout was on his way, with Hatcher guiding his career at every step. Last year he was the top-grossing touring artist in country music. □

REBA MCENTIRE

The twin-engine Hawker Siddeley jet carrying seven members of country singer Reba McEntire's band and her tour manager took off from Brown Field, south of San Diego, at 1:40 A.M. on a Saturday last March. Minutes later, the jet's wing clipped an outcropping of rock near the 3,572-foot peak of Otay Mountain east of the airfield. Investigators say the plane was going 200 miles per hour when it cartwheeled and smashed into the side of the mountain, killing all on board.

Only hours before, guitarist Chris Austin, 27, backup singer Paula Kaye Evans, 33, bassist Terry Jackson, 28, guitarist Michael Thomas, 34, drummer Tony Saputo, 34, and keyboardist Joey Cigainero, 27, had performed a 75-minute set with McEntire at San Diego's Sheraton Harbor Island Hotel. The musicians and McEntire's longtime tour manager, Jim Hammon, 40, were bound for a concert in Fort Wayne, Indiana. McEntire had skipped the flight after her husband and manager, Narvel Blackstock, 34, urged her to stay behind and get a good night's sleep in order to speed her recovery from bronchitis. McEntire planned to fly to Fort Wayne the next day. Band members Joe McGlohon, 36, and Pete Finney, 36, had taken off from Brown Field in a different plane, minutes behind the doomed jet.

McEntire, 35, the premier female vocalist in country music, appeared as scheduled at the Academy Awards nine days later. She sang "I'm Checking Out" from *Postcards from the Edge*. "I'm doing it for the band," she said beforehand. "They're checking out. They've got a new place to dwell . . . It's like God has bigger and better things for them up there." The singer, who resumed touring with a pickup band in April, set up a fund to aid the victims' families. □

WHOOPI GOLDBERG

Looking unaccustomedly regal in a floor-length black sequined gown, Whoopi Goldberg accepted her Best Supporting Actress Oscar for *Ghost*, and moved the audience when she confided, "As a little kid, I lived in the projects and you're the people I watched. I'm proud to be an actor."

Backstage at the Shrine Auditorium, she was asked whether she had learned any spiritual lesson playing the medium Oda Mae Brown in the box office smash.

"Spiritual lesson?" the irrepressible comedienne shot back. "If anything, it taught me to get a piece of the back end [Hollywood-speak for when big stars get a percentage of the gross box office receipts] and a piece of the video. That's what *Ghost* taught me." □

BILL T. JONES He moves with liquid grace and a startling range of power. Equally expressive as a choreographer, the 39-year-old New Yorker recently led his company on a tour of *Last Supper at Uncle Tom's Cabin/The Promised Land,* a three-hour work focusing on AIDS, sexism and the legacy of slavery. This fall Jones directed and choreographed *Mother of Three Sons,* a dance opera at the New York City Opera. ☐

PATRICK SWAYZE Who else can rope a calf, swan-dive into a pool, parachute from a plane, cry on cue—*and* turn a mean pirouette? Patrick Swayze, PEOPLE's 1991 *Sexiest Man Alive*, has gone from *Dirty Dancing* to *Ghost* to *Point Break* with astonishing grace. In his latest film, *City of Joy*, he plays an American doctor in poverty-stricken Calcutta.

What accounts for his undeniable appeal? His wife of 16 years, 34-year-old actress and dancer Lisa Niemi, says, "Looks only go so far. It's something in his spirit that makes him so attractive." His mother, Patsy, a dance instructor and film choreographer, has another idea: "He knows he's just an ordinary, down-home Texas kid." □

LUKE PERRY Maybe it's the dagger sideburns or the wounded puppy eyes—whatever it is that Luke Perry, star on the Fox series *Beverly Hills, 90210*, employs to hold teenage girls in thrall, he might consider throttling it back some. In a scene reminiscent of the glory days of Elvis and David Cassidy, Perry was stampeded by a frenzied mob of admirers when he appeared at a south Florida mall in August. Of the 21 fans who were injured, 13 had to be sent to area hospitals. Just three months before, when Perry appeared at a mall in Bellevue, Washington, he had to be hidden in a laundry hamper after 4,000 rushed him. Following the Florida incident, a shocked Perry tried to contact the victims who were hospitalized. He also canceled two future appearances. □

JASON PRIESTLEY Like his *90210* costar Luke Perry, Jason Priestley receives about 1,500 fan letters a week. The 22-year-old, Vancouver-born star started acting in commercials at age 4, and played an orphan on the NBC sitcom *Sister Kate*. Unlike his thoughtful, levelheaded, earnest character, Brandon Walsh, Priestley chain-smokes, whips around on a Yamaha motorcycle and a dirt bike, plays hockey with a local league and revels in bungee jumping. Basically, he says he is up for anything "if it's dangerous and life-threatening." □

ARNOLD SCHWARZENEGGER

The verdict appears to be unanimous: He's the biggest star around today. Not bad for a man who left his native land at 21 because, as he once told Studs Terkel, "I didn't like being in a little country like Austria."

As for the persistent rumors that he is interested in running for office, the star of *Terminator 2* says *nein*. Despite his work for the Republican Party and his chairmanship of the President's Council on Physical Fitness, Schwarzenegger claims the only office he's interested in is the box office—where he's doing just fine.

Schwarzenegger, 43, is married, of course, to Maria Shriver, 35, host of NBC's *First Person with Maria Shriver*. His marriage and the recent birth of the couple's second daughter have apparently turned the former bodybuilder's thoughts to women—surrounded as he is now—and attending to them. "There are some women who don't need as much," he observes. "My mother doesn't need as much. Maria is high maintenance." □

KEVIN COSTNER

He laid himself on the line for *Dances with Wolves* and waltzed away with seven Oscars. (The Sioux nation, rarely pleased with its portrayal onscreen, adopted Costner as a member of its tribal family.) In *Robin Hood* the 36-year-old actor insisted on doing many of his own stunts. Everyone seems to like Hollywood's new Mr. Right—well, maybe not *everyone*.

Perhaps "neat" was not the best word to use for Madonna's kick-ass concert. Costner visited backstage and offered the offending compliment, which was captured in a memorable cameo in *Truth or Dare*, the Madonna documentary. After he leaves, Madonna sticks a finger down her throat and makes a gagging sound. "I don't know why I was in the film," said Costner, who had no kind words for *Truth or Dare*. "They gave us tickets. She invited *us*. I don't know why she would do that."

Costner may have gotten his revenge: *Variety* reported that Madonna went after the costarring role in *The Bodyguard*, Costner's next film. Whitney Houston got the part. □

Princess Caroline of Monaco

High atop the promontory the locals call the Rock, the door to Clos Saint-Pierre would open. Princess Caroline, 34, would step from the two-story villa, her clothes, invariably black, hanging loosely on a 5'8" frame grown far thinner than her family and friends thought healthy. Her pale face was shielded by sunglasses even when skies were overcast.

Below, to the east, lies Monte Carlo, its fabled Casino overlooking a harbor crammed with luxury yachts. To the south is the locus of her grief, the place where her Italian-born husband, Stefano Casiraghi, died in October 1990. He was trapped when his boat, *Pinot di Pinot*, flipped while slamming across the waves at 100-plus miles per hour. In deference to Caroline, the principality's Christmas card that year featured not the traditional royal family portrait but rather a photograph of a decorated tree in the palace courtyard. Yet though the official mourning period ended in early January, Caroline continued to shun contact with all but family and close friends.

In any other family, Caroline would have been allowed her bereavement. But Princess Grace's 1982 death forced the First Daughter to assume the role of First Lady of Monaco as well, heading up charities and presiding over the social life that is crucial to maintaining the principality's chief asset, glamour.

Monaco is the world's second-smallest sovereign state: At 482 acres, it is larger only than Vatican City. Nestled on the coast five miles from the French-Italian border, the enclave was a Genoese stronghold in 1297 when the first

Princess Caroline and her father, Prince Rainier.

Grimaldi—Lanfranco the Spiteful—arrived dressed as a friar and by this ruse stole control of the castle. Monaco's longtime revenue stream from piracy eventually petered out, but in 1878 the famed Casino was opened, transforming the sleepy principality into a magnet for jaded aristocracy and parvenus. Eyeing the losers streaming from the tables, Somerset Maugham was moved to call Monaco "a sunny place for shady people."

Since ascending the throne in 1949, Prince Rainier III has changed that, becoming the first monarch in centuries actually to live in Monaco most of the year. He reduced the principality's dependency on gaming income, which currently accounts for less than 4 percent of Monaco's revenues. To take its place, Rainier built up the profitable tourist and convention industries and worked to make his little domain an attractive tax shelter for banks and such high-income celebrities as tennis ace Boris Becker, designer Karl Lagerfeld and opera star Placido Domingo.

His masterstroke, though, was his 1956 marriage to Hollywood icon Grace Kelly. She not only gave the principality an instant cachet, she also bore Caroline, Albert and Stephanie, thereby saving Monaco's independence. Had Rainier died without an heir (though he could have adopted one), control would have become vested in France.

Nine years ago the Land-Rover carrying Grace and Stephanie back from their weekend home careered off the serpentine road winding down to Monaco. Grace's death plunged Rainier into mourning for years. Just when the family seemed to have regained its equilibrium, Casiraghi died.

Caroline finally made an official appearance at the 24th annual Flower Arranging Competition in May. Eyes hidden by large sunglasses, her luxurious hair chopped off in a severe blunt cut, she appeared pale, tired and quite obviously strained. Since then she has resumed some official duties—and even sparked a few rumors. It seems that French actor Vincent Lindon, 31, was spotted at Caroline's secluded 19th-century farmhouse near Avignon. He was also seen shopping with her children, Andrea, 7, Charlotte, 4, and Pierre, 3, in a nearby village. Reported a workman who was refurbishing Caroline's farmhouse when Lindon was a guest: "They were not making a public spectacle of themselves at all." □

The British Royals

Prince Philip

The brash, intriguing Duke of Edinburgh celebrated his 70th birthday June 10. He's a pilot, Captain-General of the Royal Marines, international president of the World Wide Fund for Nature, an enthusiastic marksman and an unstoppable flirt. The outspoken prince is also notorious for uttering colorful but highly inappropriate remarks while going about his official duties. In Washington, D.C., commenting on the Protestant-Catholic conflict in Northern Ireland, the Prince said, "As long as they agree on conservation, I don't care what they do to each other." Somewhat less damaging was his announcement while opening a city hall annex in Vancouver: "I now declare this thing open, whatever it is."

Princess Diana and Prince Charles

Once upon a time, the world fell in love with a dashing Prince and his enchanting bride. Ten years later, Charles and Diana do not appear to be living happily ever after...

The onetime kindergarten teacher who became the world's favorite royal a decade ago turned 30 on July 1. If royalty watchers expected a demonstration of togetherness, it was not to be. Accord-

ing to some reports, Charles offered to throw her a party, but Di declined, celebrating instead with friends in London while he remained at their country house, Highgrove.

Despite the gauzy romantic imagery behind their fairy-tale marriage, Charles settled on Di not out of love but because she had a pedigree and no "past." Family confidants confirm that Charles never intended to—and never did—give up his bachelor ways and made this clear to Diana at the very outset of their marriage. In particular, these sources go on, Charles told Di she would have to accept that "certain time is set aside for Camilla"—that is, the continuation of his friendship with Camilla Parker Bowles, a former girlfriend whose husband, Andrew, is a Household Cavalry brigadier. Andrew is, conveniently, persona grata in royal circles.

Such liaisons, by no means uncommon in Britain's upper classes, usually feature the husband cavorting in London while the wife is ensconced at the family's country seat. In this case it is Diana who stays at Kensington Palace, the Waleses' London base, during the week, while Charles, 42, and Camilla, 43, see each other at their nearby properties in the idyllic, rural West of England. Some insiders believe that proximity to Camilla was a factor in Charles's acquisition of Highgrove in 1980, a year before he married Di.

For Charles, the comparisons between Camilla, a longtime friend his own age, and his younger, demure wife may be invidious. According to a royal biographer, Ann Morrow, Camilla is "everything Charles loves: worldly, fun, sporty, blond ... and, of course, very sexy. She has traveled the world, has strong opinions and likes nothing better than tramping the grouse moors in the howling wind. It's a pretty heady mixture: an attractive, well-bred woman who looks stunning in a ball gown but can call a hound to heel."

Reminders of how the Prince and his marriage are widely perceived—in the public eye, Di can do no wrong, while he goes on being boxed around the ears—are said to infuriate him. Some of the Prince's friends have retaliated by circulating stories that Di consciously manipulates domestic situations to enhance her image at the expense of her husband's. But even confirmed royalists were dismayed by Charles's conduct in the year since his polo accident. Besides his self-indulgent withdrawal from public life for four months, Charles's ongoing detachment from his family provoked widespread criticism. Though he is an avid skier, he didn't accompany his sons on their first skiing holiday. Most extraordinary of all was Charles leaving the hospital to attend an opera just as Prince William, 9, was about to be operated on for a fractured skull, suffered when he was accidentally struck with a golf club at his school, Ludgrove.

There *have* been two notable attempts at altering public perceptions of a failed marriage: The Prince did make an appearance at Wetherby, the school attended by young Prince Harry, 6. While Princess Diana shucked her shoes and gamely ran in the annual Mummies' Race, Charles smiled and clapped—and sketched the festivities in pencil. A back injury sidelined him from the equivalent Daddies' Race. And in August, Charles and Di surprised—better, stunned—palace pundits by sailing off on a 10th-anniversary cruise. The "second honeymoon" took a course similar to the first—a Mediterranean voyage—but was not as private: Charles and Di were joined by Princes William and Harry. Still, the press was ecstatic. ROMANTIC CRUISE TO GIVE LOVE A CHANCE, was the London *Daily Mirror*'s headline.

PRINCESS ANNE

Great Britain's Princess Anne officially separated in 1989 from Captain Mark Phillips, her husband of 16 years. At first the two equestrians had shared a love of horses, but Phillips was set on becoming a millionaire squire, and Anne was expanding beyond competitive riding. For years the heartily disliked Princess, who was known as Her Royal Haughtiness, turned on Fleet Street snoops and paparazzi with flared nostrils and earthy expletives. Now, at age 41, the Princess is arguably one of the most widely admired members of the family. Given her natural wit and whip-crack intelligence, Anne learned to perform her public duties with a compelling verve and passion. As president of the Save the Children Fund for 20 years, she has logged tens of thousands of gritty miles in the Third World with no primping or grandstanding.

Grown apart, the Phillipses each began to graze in lusher pastures. His name was romantically linked with, among others, a stable girl and a former Miss India. Anne reportedly tested her own charms on several men. (Although she inherited the endearing royal overbite and disappearing chin, Anne, said a friend, "can be terribly sexy, really turn it on.") In 1989 several love letters to her from Navy Commander Tim Laurence, 37, were stolen, and the incident was splashed in the press.

That was nothing compared to recent revelations about her estranged husband. Last spring, while Phillips's lawyers were busy dealing with his impending divorce settlement, the *Daily Express*, a London tabloid, broke the news in a copyrighted story that Phillips was facing a paternity suit on the other side of the world. New

Zealander Heather Tonkin, 37, a blond art teacher (and, like Phillips, an equestrian), claims that Phillips is the father of her 5-year-old daughter, Felicity. Tonkin has filed suit for maintenance in Auckland's Otahuhu District Court.

Tonkin's case is not easy to dismiss. Although Phillips has never publicly acknowledged paternity, he has, for five years, made quarterly payments to her totaling $80,000 through an agent in Sydney, Australia. The agent, James Erskine, regional director of International Management Group and a close personal friend of Phillips's, says the fees were for "equestrian consultancy."

The news broke when Tonkin apparently became angry over a magazine article suggesting that Phillips might receive as much as $2 million after his divorce from Princess Anne. Phillips does have a substantial claim, if only for his efforts in building Gatcombe Park, the royal estate, into an attractive equestrian center. Tonkin, who chose to press her claim in court after she sought a substantial cash settlement and was rebuffed, sold her story to the *Express* for $180,000.

Princess Anne has kept mum on the subject. Though a spokesman for the Princess would only comment that "this is a matter for Captain Phillips and his legal advisers," one well-connected royal watcher observed, "Mark has had it. There will be no more invitations to Buckingham Palace —and Anne's hand will be strengthened significantly." Referring to the fact that Phillips, at Queen Elizabeth's sufferance, was still residing in a cottage on the royal estate, the watcher continued, "This is all the excuse Anne needed to get Mark out of Gatcombe."

THE DUCHESS OF YORK

Every morning after the Duchess of York rolls out of bed, she looks in the mirror as part of her recent self-improvement regimen and asks, "Who loves me?" Then she reels off the names of her husband, Prince Andrew, and their daughters Beatrice, 3, and Eugenie, 1. If she wished, she might even add some of the nation's more persnickety royal watchers and a growing cadre of the British tabloid press. It sure marks a change.

Last winter, after months of a relatively blameless life (which for Sarah Ferguson, 31, means staying off the front pages), she was up to her old high-profile, low public-approval tricks again. Moreover, she was out partying while her husband was away on sea duty with the Royal Navy and British troops were risking their lives in the gulf war. All in all, her skirts were too short and the list of her indiscretions far too long. (Even

her mother-in-law, the Queen, expressed displeasure when, on a trip to New York City in 1990, Fergie took a table knife and dubbed her hostess's dog Sir Rutherford.)

Beginning last spring, the Duchess went on a crash course in image cleansing. She began trading nightlife for hearth and home and, to please the Queen, cut down on some of her club-hopping with such fast-track pals as Texas oil-heir–playboy Steve Wyatt. After getting her act together, Fergie took it on the road to New York City and Los Angeles, a combined pleasure and royal-business trip. Gone was the irrepressible good-time Duchess. In her place was the "Caring Duchess," a more slender, more chic, more subdued and certainly more discreet Sarah. She visited hospitals, made promotional speeches and took a delighted Beatrice to Disneyland. (Baby Eugenie stayed home with her nanny; Andrew was in Papua, New Guinea, to open the South Pacific Games.)

While her improved press has doubtless been gratifying, a change in her private life may have made her happier still. This past fall Lieutenant Andrew, who spent only 43 days at home last year, gave up sea duty to become a land-based helicopter instructor in Dorset. □

Matthew, left, and Gunnar.

NELSON

As the giant pink tour bus bearing the band Nelson rolls along its 145-city tour, it is met by the screeches of hundreds of teenage fans (and not a few well past puberty). The objects of their affection are a pair of baby-faced, blond-maned rockers, Matthew and Gunnar Nelson, 23, identical-twin sons of the late Rick Nelson, who inspired his own fair share of teen frenzy.

These scions of television's First Family of the '50s are carrying on a show-business legacy that stretches back four generations. Their pop-rock debut album, *After the Rain*, has sold nearly 2 million copies, with two of its songs making *Billboard*'s Top 10 and "Love and Affection"

soaring to No. 1. Says their actress sister, Tracy, 27, who has mother-henned Gunnar and Matthew since their father's death in 1985 and even bankrolled them in lean times: "I'm constantly amazed at my brothers. These guys have every right to be so screwed up, and they've come through."

Not, to be sure, without grief and pain. "We come from the granddaddy of dysfunctional families," says Matthew. It was because of their lamentable family history, Gunnar adds, that they titled their album *After the Rain*. "Right before our parents got separated in 1981," he says, "my mom started drinking really heavily. She went to AA, but there were drunken battles that none of us will ever forget." Their relationship with their mother, the former Kris Harmon, became so difficult and their admiration for their father so deep, that they moved in with him in the fall of 1985, on their 18th birthday.

That was just three months before Rick's chartered DC-3 crashed on a New Year's Eve outside

DeKalb, Texas, killing the 45-year-old singer and six others. It remains a point of extreme bitterness with his children that Rick was initially accused of causing the explosion by freebasing cocaine during the flight because traces of the drug were found in his blood. Subsequent investigation by the FAA exonerated the singer, finding that the explosion was caused by a faulty heating system.

Rick's death hit the twins especially hard. They hadn't seen much of their road-warrior father for most of their lives, so those last three months with him were profoundly important to them. They suffered another blow less than two years later, when a bitter custody battle erupted over Sam, then 13, the youngest of Rick's four children. When it appeared that their mother, Kris, was coming apart, her brother, actor Mark Harmon, backed by his sister Kelly, the Tic-Tac pitchwoman, and his wife, actress Pam Dawber, petitioned for custody of Sam. The clash tore the families apart: Matthew, Gunnar and Tracy supported Kris, while Sam's maternal grandparents, football star Tom Harmon (now deceased) and his wife, Elyse Knox, backed Mark. The conflict ended abruptly when Kris's attorney persistently questioned Pam Dawber about whether she had experimented with drugs. The next day, the Harmon contingent dropped the case.

Sam remains with his mother, who claims she has been sober since 1985. She is remarried to TV producer Mark (*St. Elsewhere*) Tinker. Kris, 46, readily admits her problems now but offers an explanation for her deterioration. "There were four kids to be raised," she says, "and Rick wasn't home a whole lot." Money was a problem too; Rick died heavily in debt (brother David is settling his estate), and his four kids inherited just $25,000 apiece in insurance money.

Over time, the drinking and the family strife created a rift between Kris and her twin sons that has been very slow to heal. "We've kind of grown apart over the years," Gunnar says softly, "but I would like nothing more than to be friends." He agrees that his father's absences caused marital strain. "It was her experience with music that alienated them," says Gunnar. "Pop was out on the road the whole time, and I think music took the form of another woman. It created a lot of hostility. I tried to explain to [my mother] that the music business has changed a lot. But that's why she was so down on us."

The twins' botched upbringing is responsible for their determination to avoid drugs and alcohol entirely. "We got to see the ravages firsthand," says Matthew, who is 45 minutes older than Gunnar and usually the spokesman for the pair. Whatever problems they've faced with their parents, the twins—and Tracy—retain a strong sense of family tradition. All three credit their grandmother, the redoubtable Harriet Hilliard Nelson, clan matriarch, with imbuing them with a strong sense of heritage.

On their tour, the twins returned to some of the scenes of Rick's concert triumphs years before. They play only their own songs, though, flatly refusing to cover any of their father's numbers. "Nobody can do Ricky Nelson better than Ricky Nelson," says Matthew. "Anything we could do would be a parody. It would be disrespectful."

Ironically, in one respect there seems to be a case of like father like at least one son: Matthew has reportedly been seeing Erin Everly, the 25-year-old daughter of Everly brother Don, since her marriage to heavy-metal rocker Axl Rose was annulled. Matthew didn't want to talk about the fledgling romance, but his mother Kris called it "amazing. When I heard Matthew was going with Erin, I said, 'Matthew, Pop used to date her mother!'" □

MARTINA NAVRATILOVA

I
n 1990 Martina Navratilova won her record-breaking ninth Wimbledon singles championship —more than any other man or woman in history. At the moment of victory, she raised her arms, sank to her knees and scanned the crowd for longtime companion Judy Nelson, the honey-blond former Texas beauty queen who six years before had left a husband and two children to move in with her. As their eyes met, both women burst into tears.

What a difference a year makes. This past summer, as the 34-year-old Navratilova made another run at Wimbledon history, Nelson, who is 45, was conspicuously absent. In the spring, she had received a perfunctory letter from Navratilova, officially ending their seven-year relationship. Shortly before Wimbledon, Nelson filed suit in a Texas court, asking for 50 percent of all money and property Navratilova has acquired since 1984. After failed negotiations with Navratilova, Nelson produced a 15-page "non-marital cohabitation agreement" that she and Navratilova signed in 1986—which her lawyer said might entitle her to between $5 million and $10 million.

"For years I have supported and assisted Martina, sacrificing many of my own personal goals in the process," Nelson said. "She has left me and pursued another relationship. She is now refusing to abide by the very terms of the partnership agreement and left my life in disarray."

It was an ugly end to what, by all accounts, had been the happiest of alternative marriages. Navratilova first met Judy Hill Nelson in 1982 at a tournament in Fort Worth, where Judy's son Edward was a ball boy. They met again, two years later, at a tournament in Dallas. Local papers soon reported that Nelson and her husband, Edward, a prominent internist, had become friendly with the tennis star. Navratilova, who had previously lived with lesbian author Rita Mae Brown, invited the Nelsons to Wimbledon. Edward declined; Judy never came home.

When Navratilova and Nelson returned to Fort Worth, it was as a couple. Together, they moved into a costly town house. Nelson's husband gained custody of their two sons in a nondisputed agreement, but Navratilova sometimes pitched in to drive car pools for the boys. A few years later she gave Judy's son Eddie a Porsche 944, which she had won in a tournament.

Soon after the relationship began, Nelson and part of her family joined the ranks of coaches and friends who made up Navratilova's travel entourage. Judy's brother signed on as director of the Martina Youth Foundation. Nelson's mother helped Judy with designs for Navratilova's new clothing line, MN.

According to Nelson, both she and Navratilova wanted the now-disputed partnership agreement to express "our relationship as equals. Just as we shared views on the environment and animal rights, it was one more issue we agreed on. Maybe I was out designing clothes and she was out practicing tennis, but we wanted it clear that we were equal partners."

Navratilova now claims naïveté about the agreement. To buttress her assertion that the partnership was less than official, her lawyer produced undated, handwritten notes she made, apparently before the signing. In part, they read: "Judy gets the Rolls-Royce . . . her horse (Cat's Ghost or the black stallion she's looking for now), $30,000 for every year we live together, starting in March 1984."

Nelson willingly led the life of a globe-trotting tennis spouse. About nine months a year, she

Martina and Judy in 1985. Navratilova had agreed that Nelson will have "visitation rights to the pets."

accompanied Navratilova on the circuit; the rest of the time was divided between a Trump Plaza apartment in New York City and houses in Fort Worth and Aspen, where they moved a few years ago. Things began going badly at the Toray Pan Pacific Open in Tokyo last January. "I was upset about some things that had transpired, and I told [Martina] if these things were true that we needed to be separated," said Nelson. "She more or less just said, 'Okay, then, goodbye.' When we got home, she left. Later she called me and said, 'We're through.' I was devastated."

Did Martina leave Judy for somebody else? Nelson snapped bitterly, "What do *you* think? Martina doesn't like to be alone."

Navratilova was reportedly keeping company with 35-year-old former U.S. ski team star Cindy Nelson, now director of skiing at Vail and Beaver Creek. (Through a spokeswoman, Cindy Nelson denied that she had anything other than a friendship with Navratilova.) "I did not leave Judy for a younger woman or anyone else," said Martina. "We simply parted."

If there's one thing the parting certainly hasn't been, it's simple. Early in September, Navratilova and Nelson appeared in a Fort Worth court, but attempts to reach a settlement reportedly stalled because Nelson refused to agree not to write a book about their relationship. "It's an American right, my freedom of speech," argued Nelson. □

THE L.A.P.D. AND RODNEY KING

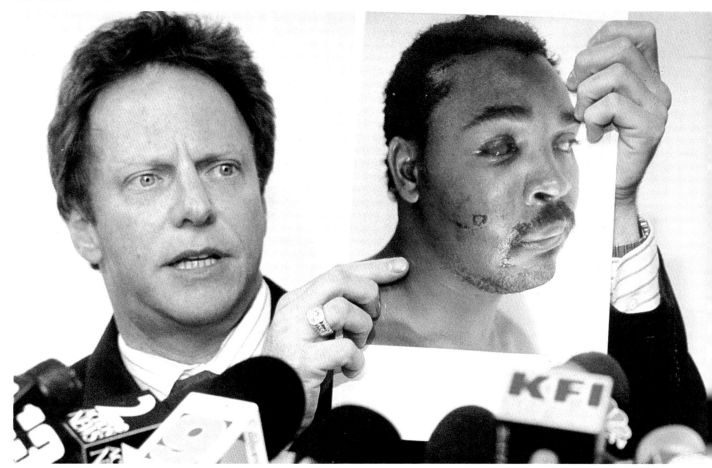

A little after midnight one Sunday in March, George Holliday was jolted awake by the scream of police sirens and a helicopter buzzing over his San Fernando Valley apartment. Rubbing the sleep from his eyes, he grabbed his new camcorder and began to tape the nightmarish scene outside his living room window: While more than a half dozen police officers stood by, at least three other cops savagely beat and kicked a black man who lay helpless on the ground.

Holliday admitted that initially he did not fully appreciate the brutality of what he saw through his viewfinder. "It was almost like I was watching something on a tiny television—images more than reality," he said. Holliday, manager of a plumbing business, heard nothing about the incident on the local news and assumed nobody would care about his tape. Nevertheless, talking about the incident with his wife, Eugenia, who had witnessed part of the violence, he felt something ought to be done. He called his local police precinct, described the attack and politely inquired about the disposition of the case. The desk officer told him, in effect, to mind his own business. The brush-off convinced Holliday to go public.

He called KTLA, a Los Angeles TV station, and dropped off the cassette. The broadcast of the tape that night on the 10 o'clock news ignited a fire storm. Within days, as the tape appeared again and again on network news shows, the entire country recoiled in horror. The *Los Angeles Times* called the tape "America's Ugliest Home Video." Even Daryl Gates, L.A.'s hard-line police chief, decried the incident as "two minutes that will go down in infamy." Gates did argue that the attack on Rodney King, 25, a construction worker who recently served time for a liquor-

From left, clockwise: King's lawyer with a photo of him; Officers Laurence Powell and Ted Briseno; Chief Daryl Gates; Officer Timothy Wind; Sgt. Stacey Koon.

store holdup and who police claimed had resisted arrest, was an "aberration." But critics of the Los Angeles Police Department, who have long accused its officers of persistent brutality against minorities, vigorously disagreed.

In defense of the officers, L.A. police officials contended that King, of Altadena, California, had been spotted going 115 mph in his Hyundai Excel on the Foothill Freeway. (A Hyundai spokesman says, however, that the unsporty Excel has never topped 100 mph.) When officers gave chase, police say, King took off. King insists there was no chase and that his only offense was going 45 in a 35-mph zone.

Whatever the facts, the pursuing officers, none of whom was black, finally surrounded King in front of Holliday's apartment in Lake View Terrace. After King emerged from the car and lay down on the ground, eyewitnesses reported, one cop jolted him twice, apparently with a Taser stun gun, which delivers a 50,000-volt electric charge. Then the beating began: All told, there were more than 55 blows struck with metal nightsticks, and as many as seven kicks. A team of doctors assembled by defense lawyers for King found that his injuries included a cracked eye socket, a fractured cheekbone, a broken right ankle and numerous facial lacerations. Many of the fillings had been knocked from his teeth.

The county district attorney's office initiated a grand-jury probe and lawyers for King have prepared an $83 million civil rights suit against the L.A.P.D. An independent bipartisan commission appointed to investigate the incident charged the L.A.P.D. with tolerating racism, excessive use of force and lax discipline. The commission recommended sweeping reforms and, while not directly blaming Gates, urged that the department "commence the transition to a new chief of police." After some hedging, Gates finally announced that he would retire as of April 1992, provided a successor has been named.

Sergeant Stacey C. Koon, 40, and Officers Laurence M. Powell, 28, Timothy E. Wind, 30, and Theodore J. Briseno, 38, were indicted on felony charges, including assault with a deadly weapon. Six of the 21 L.A.P.D. officers who stood by as King was beaten have been indefinitely relieved of duty, and four more were suspended for up to 22 days without pay. □

WILLIAM KENNEDY SMITH

S enator Edward Kennedy later called it a "traditional Easter weekend." At the family's Palm Beach, Florida, retreat, in the early hours after Good Friday, Teddy and his younger son, Patrick, 23, picked up a woman they had met at a bar, and another woman claimed she was raped on the grounds of the Kennedy estate.

After the alleged victim went to the police, authorities moved so cautiously that cynics thought they detected a cover-up. For those who remembered previous Kennedy embarrassments, the Palm Beach story seemed all too familiar.

This time, suspicions focused not on the Senator himself but on William Kennedy Smith, his 30-year-old nephew. A fourth-year medical student at Georgetown University in Washington, D.C., Smith was identified by the Palm Beach police department as the prime suspect in the reported assault. Once a low-profile Kennedy cousin, young Willy (son of Jean Kennedy Smith and the late Stephen Smith) found himself hounded by TV cameras and plastered all over the tabloids.

Sometime after midnight on Holy Saturday, Teddy, Patrick Kennedy, the youngest of his three children and a Rhode Island State Representative, and Willy Smith appeared at Au Bar, a chichi Palm Beach nightspot. When the bar closed at 3 A.M., Patrick invited Michele Cassone, a 27-year-old waitress he had met on the dance floor, to come have a drink with him and his father.

Driving her own car, Cassone followed the Kennedys' white convertible, with Patrick at the wheel, back to La Guerida, the family mansion. While Patrick and Cassone chatted in the living room, the Senator disappeared. When he reappeared, according to Cassone, it was without trousers; he seemed to be wearing only a long-tailed shirt. "I got totally weirded out," says Cassone, who announced that she was leaving.

Instead, Patrick suggested they sit on the seawall. After putting on his trousers, Ted joined them, then she and Patrick took a walk on the beach. Sometime between 4:30 and 5 A.M., Cassone drove away from La Guerida—never suspecting, she says, that any sort of sexual assault had taken place.

The story of what happened elsewhere on the estate that evening remains elusive. Authorities have released few details about their investigation, and no one seems to have seen Smith and the alleged victim at the Kennedy compound.

According to a source who works for the City of Palm Beach (and who spoke with the *Fort Lauderdale Sun-Sentinel*), when Smith and the young woman arrived at the family compound, they decided to walk on the beach. By this account, Smith took off his clothes and waded into the surf. While he was swimming, the woman began walking back to the house. After she left the beach, she claimed, Smith grabbed her ankle from behind, tripping her, and then sexually assaulted her.

The source told the *Sun-Sentinel* that Smith later followed his visitor into the house and tried to convince her that there had been no rape. Reportedly the woman telephoned a friend, who agreed to meet her at the Kennedy compound. As the weekend wore on, the Kennedys gave little sign that anything out of the ordinary had occurred. At La Guerida, Teddy hosted an intimate Saturday lunch for a former girlfriend. According to one guest, the mood was light; everyone present, including Jean Smith, carried on as though nothing had happened during the night. The Senator, who attended Mass at St. Edward's Catholic Church on Sunday, also made appearances at a local bar and restaurant.

By late Saturday morning, the woman had notified police. She appeared at Humana Hospital's rape center later that afternoon in the company of a detective and was treated for minor injuries and subjected to forensic testing. In a

resort town where there are few secrets, the name of Smith's alleged victim quickly circulated. A dark-haired, attractive 29-year-old, she is well-known to patrons of watering holes like Au Bar. The stepdaughter of a wealthy industrialist, the alleged victim, who is unmarried, lives with her 2-year-old daughter in nearby Jupiter. Once employed as a clerk at the *Palm Beach Post*, she had attended Rollins College and held jobs at a law firm, a Methodist church and Walt Disney World.

Willy, the second of Stephen and Jean Kennedy Smith's four children, was raised in New York City, where Stephen Smith was in charge of the Kennedy fortune. Smith's real job, though, was protector of the Kennedy family itself: It was he who mobilized the spin control after Chappaquiddick and who became his nephew David Kennedy's legal guardian when he was struggling with heroin addiction. While the late Smith was reputed to be a womanizer, his wife, Jean, eighth child of Joseph and Rose Kennedy, is considered a model of public dignity, a low-profile cosmopolite committed to charity fund raising.

A 1983 graduate of Duke University, Willy worked briefly as an investment banker before entering Georgetown University Medical School, where he championed on-campus rights for women and minorities and designed a program to help physicians interact with terminally ill children. Although he has now graduated from Georgetown, Willy has not been able to begin his residency at the University of New Mexico School of Medicine as planned.

Last May, Willy Smith —who called it "an outrageous lie"—was charged by Palm Beach police with involuntary sexual battery (as rape is termed under Florida law). Prosecutor Moira Lasch poured on the heat from the start, even publicly criticizing Ted Kennedy for making extensive changes in his police statement. Later she dropped a bombshell on the defense by asking Palm Beach Judge Mary Lupo to admit testimony from three women who claim Smith sexually assaulted them. Lasch, who is under a court-imposed gag order, has taken a lot of criticism for publicly filing the depositions of the three women, none of whom ever pressed criminal charges. While the press reported details of the depositions, Smith's lawyers were prevented by the court's gag order from responding publicly to the charges. They will have to wait for the trial. □

JEFFREY DAHMER

Jeffrey Dahmer

prompting Dahmer to leap up from the sofa, screaming like a terrified animal. When Mueller opened the refrigerator he found a human head sitting next to a box of baking soda. As the officers led the handcuffed Dahmer outside, neighbors—who say he attracted stray cats—heard him meowing.

Over the next several hours, a grim procession of officers wearing oxygen masks and protective suits turned up the remains of 11 men from the slaughterhouse that was Dahmer's home. Three more heads were found in a lift-top freezer. Five skulls, apparently scraped clean, were stowed in a box and a filing cabinet; two more were stashed on a closet shelf. Police found five full skeletons and the remains of six other bodies—three of which were in a chemical-filled, 57-gallon plastic drum in the bedroom. Body parts were stored about the apartment—including bones in cardboard boxes and decomposed hands and a genital organ in a lobster pot—as were bottles of acid, chloroform and formaldehyde and various tools, including three electric saws.

Officers Robert Rauth and Rolf Mueller were on a routine patrol of Milwaukee's rundown west side on a scorching July night. Cruising near North 25th Street, they saw a man, apparently dazed, running toward them. A pair of handcuffs dangled from his wrist. Tracy Edwards, 32, flagged the patrol car, pointed to the Oxford Apartments up the street and said that the man in apartment 213 had a big knife under the bed and was trying to kill him.

Rauth and Mueller, veteran cops, were unprepared for the chamber of horrors that awaited them behind the door of apartment 213. A putrid stench assaulted their noses as 31-year-old Jeffrey Dahmer—pale, soft-spoken, his breath reeking of beer—politely let them in. Mueller headed for the bedroom, where a Polaroid camera lay on the bed. There was indeed a butcher knife under the bed. But what caught Mueller's eye were the photographs spilling out of the highboy. They showed homosexual acts, men in various stages of undress—and corpse after corpse, bodies mutilated and dismembered, including one eaten away from the nipples down, apparently by acid.

With a shock, Mueller realized the pictures had been taken in that very room. After scrutinizing another grisly photo, he ran to the kitchen area,

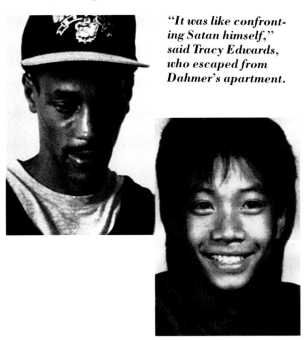

"It was like confronting Satan himself," said Tracy Edwards, who escaped from Dahmer's apartment.

Konerak Sinthasomphone was reportedly killed after police left him with Dahmer. His family is suing the city of Milwaukee, alleging police racism was to blame for the boy's death.

Steven Hicks

Joseph Bradehoft

Edward Smith

Oliver Lacy

Errol Lindsey

Dahmer confessed to the murders of the 11 victims whose remains were found in the apartment and later to six others that may date back as far as 1978. Dahmer admitted luring his victims—most of them black and homosexual —from shopping malls, bus stops and bars by offering them money to pose for pictures at his apartment. There he drugged them with sedatives, strangled and dismembered them. Dahmer also hinted at a taste for human flesh. Inside the freezer were packed lungs, intestines, a kidney, a liver, a heart—the latter, he said, had been saved "to eat later." There was no food in apartment 213, only condiments.

At first, Dahmer seemed to have an ordinary, even banal background. He was known as a mild-mannered man who worked in a chocolate factory. Eventually, as reporters interviewed family and acquaintances, a portrait emerged of a disturbed young man—an alcoholic, a homosexual who despised gays and a convicted child molester.

Born in Milwaukee and raised in the well-to-do community of Bath, Ohio, just outside Akron, Dahmer was just 8 when he was sexually abused by a man in the neighborhood. At Revere High School in nearby Richfield, where Dahmer played tennis and clarinet, he was considered bright but was unwilling to apply himself. "He had a bizarre sense of humor," says classmate John Backderf. "He bleated like a sheep in class, had fake epileptic seizures in the hallways. I don't remember having a normal conversation with him." He developed a ritual walk to the school bus: four steps forward, two back, four forward, one back, day after day, never deviating.

Dahmer began drinking heavily, often consuming several beers before going to school. A preoccupation with death and torture led schoolmates to wonder if he was dabbling in the occult. A neighbor walking in the woods behind the Dahmers' house came upon a mutilated dog carcass. The head was mounted on a stick next

Richard Guerrero

David Thomas

Curtis Straughter

Tony Hughes

Jeremiah Weinberger

Ernest Miller

Matt Turner

Ricky Beeks

Anthony Sears

42

to a wooden cross. The body, skinned and gutted, was nailed to a nearby tree. (Dahmer's stepmother, Shari Dahmer, said that young Jeffrey —who developed a keen interest in chemistry after receiving an introductory set from his chemist father—"liked to use acid to scrape the meat off dead animals.")

By his senior year, Dahmer's mother, Joyce, and his father, Lionel, were in the throes of a bitter divorce in which they fought over custody of their younger son, David, then 12. After the separation, Joyce returned to Wisconsin with David. "Jeffrey was left all alone in the house with no money, no food and a broken refrigerator," said Shari, who married Lionel after his divorce. "The desertion really affected him."

Dahmer has now confessed that he committed his first murder that year. He picked up a 19-year-old hitchhiker, Steven Hicks. Dahmer invited the youth to the house in Bath to drink beer, then bludgeoned and strangled him with a barbell before dismembering the body, cutting up the pieces and scattering them in the woods. Dahmer drew a map of the area for investigators who have already dug up about 50 bones, many tentatively identified as human vertebra or rib fragments.

After attending Ohio State for a few months, Dahmer dropped out and enlisted in the Army in December 1978. Posted to West Germany, he was still the quiet loner, except during drinking binges when he would become increasingly moody and defiant. Lying in bed, with headphones blasting Black Sabbath and other heavy-metal music, Dahmer would guzzle martinis until he passed out. Finally, in 1981, he was given an early discharge. Later that year, he moved to the Milwaukee suburb of West Allis to live with his paternal grandmother, Catherine. He worked for a downtown blood bank before taking a job in 1985 with the Ambrosia Chocolate Company, where he was a stock clerk.

In 1986 Dahmer was arrested for lewd and lascivious behavior after urinating in front of some children. He began picking up lovers at gay bars—all the while denying his homosexuality and telling acquaintances he detested gays. He was fascinated by horror movies such as *Friday the 13th* and *A Nightmare on Elm Street*. Family members recalled finding bones in the trash and a chemical-filled vat in the basement.

At the time, Dahmer insisted he was stripping flesh from animal carcasses. Recently he admitted that beginning in 1985, he had killed three men at his grandmother's home. Those bodies were apparently disposed of—save for the skull of victim Anthony Sears, 24, which was kept as a souvenir and found in the apartment on 25th Street.

Dahmer was arrested in 1988 for fondling a 13-year-old Laotian boy and offering him cash to pose for nude photos. Despite a request by the prosecuting attorney for a longer sentence during which Dahmer could be placed in programs for alcoholics and sex offenders, the judge ordered a one-year prison term that allowed him to leave for his job and receive psychological treatment as an outpatient. Released after 10 months in March 1990, he met regularly with his overworked probation officer, but only at her office and not at his home, which is usually required. Dahmer's stepmother told reporters that his stint in prison had changed him for the worse.

Dahmer killed three black men over the next year. By May, the murderous rampage accelerated. Shortly after midnight one night, two women saw Dahmer chasing a 14-year-old Asian boy, naked and with blood on his buttocks, down the alley behind the apartment house. When police arrived, they told the women to go home. The boy, a Laotian named Konerak Sinthasomphone, was dazed and apparently unable to respond. Dahmer convinced the cops that he and the boy were gay lovers having a spat. Konerak's remains were found amid the carnage at the apartment. He was the brother of the Laotian boy Dahmer had molested three years earlier.

Dahmer claimed four more victims in the next seven weeks. First was 20-year-old runaway Matt Turner, whom Dahmer picked up at a Chicago bus terminal and lured back to his apartment. Then followed Chicago resident Jeremiah Weinberger, 24. Dahmer strangled former high school track star Oliver Lacy, 23, before having anal sex with the corpse. It was Lacy's heart that Dahmer saved to eat later. In July, Dahmer was fired from his job at Ambrosia for chronic absenteeism. Three days later a neighbor heard the whine of a power saw; Dahmer, it appears, was at work on his latest victim, 25-year-old Joseph Bradehoft.

Dahmer, held on $1 million cash bond, was charged with first-degree murder for four of the killings he initially confessed to, each of which carries a mandatory life sentence. His lawyer hired a forensic psychologist to lay the ground for an insanity plea. Under Wisconsin law, Dahmer could then skip an initial trial and move to an insanity hearing before a jury.

"There's no doubt he's insane," said Lionel, who visited his son in prison. Still, Lionel insists, his son "was not born a monster. He is not a monster."

Dahmer's high school classmate John Backderf sees it differently. He recalled a recent gathering in which he and other classmates talked about their days at Revere High. "You remember Jeffrey Dahmer?" one of them asked. Replied another: "Oh, he's probably a mass murderer." □

A Story of Incest
MARILYN VAN DERBUR

Francis S. Van Derbur was a millionaire socialite and a pillar of the Denver community; Marilyn, the youngest of his four daughters, was a golden-haired beauty, a straight-A student and an AAU swimming champ. In 1957, when she was 20, she became Miss America.

Her father, a handsome, intelligent man, was president of the Denver Area Boy Scout Council and helped establish Denver's Cleo Wallace Village for Handicapped Children. But there was a secret side to him. From the time she was 5 until she was 18, Marilyn says her father molested her.

"We had all the trappings of a perfect family," Marilyn says now. "Wealth, social status, a handsome father and lovely mother." So perfect was the illusion that Marilyn completely repressed any knowledge of sexual violation by her father until she was 24, when a former youth minister from her Presbyterian church broke down her guard.

"People ask me why I didn't tell what was happening to me," she notes. "It was because I perceived no way out. A young child tells on her father and what happens? She's taken away from her family. Her father goes to jail. The family is destroyed, and the message is, 'It's all your fault.'

"In order to survive, I split into a day child, who giggled and smiled, and a night child, who lay awake in a fetal position, only to be pried apart by my father. Until I was 24, the day child had no conscious knowledge of the night child. During the day, no embarrassing or angry glances ever passed between my father and me. I had no rage toward him at all, because I had no conscious knowledge of what he was doing to me." Still, she recalls, "I was always afraid of him. Just a look from him would terrify me."

There were small signs of trouble. Young Marilyn couldn't stand to play with dolls. She didn't like to be touched or hugged. And she had a desperate need to excel—in school, at sports, in all things—just to have some control over her life. In 1955, while home for Christmas vacation

from the University of Colorado, she went into her parents' bedroom to say goodnight. "My father pulled me down to him," she reports. "I pushed away from him with such anger. That was the day child reacting, still without knowledge of the night child. He never violated me again."

Francis Van Derbur and Marilyn in 1956

45

After Marilyn Van Derbur was crowned Miss America, she threw herself into her duties, driven, as always. After her reign was up, she returned to school and was graduated Phi Beta Kappa.

Working as the spokeswoman for AT&T on the *Bell Telephone Hour*, Marilyn was in Los Angeles to film a commercial. During a lunch with her former youth minister, he somehow punctured the wall she had unconsciously erected to hide her shame. The story of incest, buried for so long, finally came out. He persuaded her to call the one person she most feared would learn her secret.

Larry Atlar had been her first real boyfriend. "I was 15, a sophomore in high school, and he was a senior. I loved him from the moment I laid eyes on him. I was safe with Larry," Marilyn says. "I had loved Larry with all my heart for nine years, but I kept running away from him without understanding why." In 1961 she married someone else, but the marriage lasted only three months.

The morning after Marilyn called Larry, he flew to Los Angeles. Her revelations cleared up a great deal for him. They dated for two more years, while Marilyn struggled with her fears about marriage. Finally Larry said to her, "Why don't we try being married for a week or two, and then if you want to leave, that's okay." They were married on February 14, 1964.

As a child, incest had colored Marilyn's life in small, unremarked, ambiguous ways. As an adult, the effects grew progressively worse. Eight years after she and Larry were married, Marilyn became pregnant. In the delivery room, she was told that the baby was in a difficult breech position.

"I had told Larry that I'd consider anesthesia only if the baby or I were near death," Marilyn recalls. "For me, sleep is when a man could do anything he wants with you and you have no power. I have never fallen asleep naturally. From age 18, I have taken a sleeping pill or lain awake. So I locked my eyes with Larry's and had a perfect, natural delivery."

Jennifer was their miracle baby, but when she turned 5, Marilyn was overcome by uncontrollable fits of sobbing and told Larry, "I don't love her anymore." It took 10 years for her to understand that in Jennifer she was seeing herself as a 5-year-old. Around the same time, Marilyn began experiencing attacks of paralysis. Doctors could find nothing physically wrong with her. She saw a psychiatrist, then decided she had to talk to her father.

Confronting him was the most difficult thing she had ever done. When she told him so, he excused himself immediately and disappeared upstairs. He returned, and Marilyn knew instinctively he'd gone to get one of the guns he always kept around the house.

"I talked for almost 20 minutes," Marilyn says, "and my father didn't deny anything. He said, 'If I had known what this would do to you, I never would have done it.' I didn't believe it then, and I don't believe it now."

After their conversation, her father pulled out the gun. He told her if she had come in any other way—she assumed he meant if she had publicly exposed him—he would have killed himself. "I believe if he had used the gun," says Marilyn, "he would have killed us both. From that day on, we never spoke of it again."

Marilyn knew she hadn't been the family's only incest victim: Early on, after revealing her secret to her older sister Gwen, she had seen the blood drain from Gwen's face. "Oh, no," Marilyn remembers her saying. "I thought I was the only one."

In 1984, with her daughter Jennifer entering puberty, Marilyn became totally dysfunctional, suffering from anxiety so acute her career as a motivational speaker came to a complete halt. "Larry thought if Gwen were to fly to Denver and talk about her violation, maybe I would go into a rage at my father and begin to heal," Marilyn recalls. "Gwen told me her story in vivid detail. I cried for her. The anguish was as fresh as if it had been the previous day." Two weeks later, when her mother called, Marilyn told her that she wasn't doing very well and that she had gone to a psychiatrist. "I knew that my father had heard me because he always listened in on the extension. That night he suffered a fatal heart attack. I felt it was my fault. I had told."

For the next seven years, Marilyn spent several hours a week in therapy. As part of the healing process, she spoke with each member of her family, including her mother.

Gwendolyn "Boots" Olinger Van Derbur was overwhelmed by disbelief the night Marilyn told her that for 13 years she had been sexually abused by her father. "The worst moment of my life was hearing that," says Boots, "worse even than losing Van. I didn't believe her at first. I didn't think she was lying. I thought she was imagining." In time, especially after her daughter Gwen said she too had been abused, Boots came to accept the truth.

"Marilyn hadn't been real well," she says. "Then when she told me, I kind of put two and two together." Following Marilyn's revelation, Boots recalled her husband going into the girls' rooms, ostensibly to help them get to sleep. "He would come back and say, 'Boy, the girls will sure sleep good now. I just gave them a good back rub.' It never occurred to me to question that," she says. "In those days we didn't even think about those things.

"Marilyn often asks me what would I have done if I had known," says Boots. "I'm sure I certainly would have done something about it—any mother would. I just don't know exactly what."

For all that, Boots recalls her 55 years of marriage as "a perfect life." With her support, the Van Derbur family gave $240,000 to start the Adult Incest Survivors Program at Denver's Kempe National Center for Prevention of and Treatment for Child Abuse and Neglect. Yet when Marilyn asked her mother to speak at a Kempe meeting, Boots was reluctant, fearful of damaging her beloved husband's reputation. "I didn't want to be a party to it," she admits. "But everyone told me how much good would come of it, the thousands of people it's going to help, you've just got to go along with it. I'll just hold my head high, and I'll remember the good things he did," she says. "I can't let it ruin my life."

Last May, after two years of working with the Kempe Center, the former Miss America told an audience of 35 the grimly inspiring story of what she calls "the greatest accomplishment of my life—surviving incest." Although none of her sisters could be there, 17 other members of her family stood together when she acknowledged the humiliation.

"My goal now is to make the word *incest* speakable and to take away the stigma we attach to it," says Marilyn. "We have to figure out how to stop these violators and how to help their families heal." □

The Van Derbur daughters in 1940, from left: Nancy, 5, Marilyn, 3, Val, 7, and Gwen, 9.

PAMELA SMART

When Pamela Wojas and Gregg
Smart met at a party during the college Christmas break five years ago, they seemed an ideal
match. The two teenagers loved good times and
rock and roll; Pam thought that Gregg, with his
shoulder-length hair, looked like Jon Bon Jovi.
Three and a half years later—after Gregg had
cut his hair and gone to work for the Nashua,
New Hampshire, life insurance firm that employed his father and Pam had taken a job as
media-services director for a nearby school district
—the two married. Gregg planned to celebrate
their first anniversary with a big party, then take
Pam away on a Florida vacation, a reward for his
banner year as a salesman.

They never had that party. On the evening of
May 1, 1990, after returning from work to the
couple's Derry, New Hampshire, town house,
24-year-old Gregg Smart was killed by a single
shot to the head with a .38-caliber revolver.
When Pam, who had been at a school board
meeting, arrived home about an hour and a half
later and saw Gregg's body in the foyer, she ran
from unit to unit in the complex, frightening
neighbors with her screams. Three days later she
led Gregg's parents, Judy and Bill Smart, in a
tender farewell ceremony, leaving roses on her
husband's grave.

Her time as a sympathetic widow proved brief.
Nine months after the shooting, Pamela Smart,
23, went on trial as an accomplice in the first-
degree murder of her husband. The gunman,
said police, was 16-year-old William Flynn,
Pam's lover.

From the beginning, police said, there were
flaws in Pam's story. The home had been ran-
sacked, and Pam told police that close to $300 in
jewelry and some compact discs were missing.
But investigators doubted that burglars would
have chosen the Smart home, whose entry was in
full view of other town houses in the complex, or
that they would have struck at night, when
people tend to be home. Besides, robbers in the
area rarely carry firearms. Interviewed by reporters again and again, Pam challenged the doubt-
ers. "I'm absolutely convinced," she told the
Derry News, "that someone was burglarizing
our home and Gregg just walked in."

A month later, the case had taken a different
turn, with the trail leading some 30 miles east-
ward to Winnacunnet High School in Hampton,
just a parking lot away from Pam's media-services
office. An 18-year-old Seabrook youth overheard
some of his teenage friends saying that they had
murdered Gregg Smart. Flynn and two friends
had driven out to the Smarts' home that night.
Flynn shot Smart while one of the other youths
held the victim. The third drove the getaway car.

Authorities charged that Smart lured Flynn
into her bed and then persuaded him to recruit
three friends—Patrick Randall, 17, Vance
Lattime, 18, and Raymond Fowler, 19—to kill
her husband. (Fowler was arrested on charges
that he had been involved in an earlier, unsuccessful attempt, when Flynn got lost en route
to the Smart home.) Using testimony by Flynn,
Randall and Lattime—all of whom cut deals
with the state—prosecutors laid out a chilling
scenario.

Smart met Flynn in the fall of 1989 at Winnacunnet, where they cultivated their mutual interest in heavy-metal music. Before long the two
were passing love notes in the school and having
sex in her Honda CRX. Flynn had vivid memories of his first sexual encounter, which he found
himself obliged to recount in court. Sitting tensely
in the witness box, he described how, as a sophomore at nearby Winnacunnet High School, he
had visited the school district's media director,
Pamela Smart, at her condo one night when her
husband was away. Smart, then 22 and an adviser of an alcohol- and drug-awareness program
at the school, sat down with him to watch the
steamy film *9½ Weeks* on her VCR. Afterward
she led him upstairs, where she did a striptease
like the one performed by Kim Basinger in the
movie. Then, to the thump of Van Halen's "Black
& Blue," they had sex. Returning to the 9½

Pam and Gregg Smart at their wedding in 1989.

room and caught her having sex with Flynn. Pierce said Pam was unhappy in her marriage but did not see divorce as a solution because she feared Gregg would win the right to their property and that he would be unwilling to let her go as she tried to establish a new life. Pierce said she heard Pam and her teenage lover plotting to kill Gregg.

But it wasn't until the boys were arrested that Pierce, who had remained close to Pam, agreed to help set a trap for her. "It was really bothering me that Pam had her husband killed," she told a television interviewer. "Her lover was in jail, and she didn't care. And how was I supposed to believe that she was actually my friend? I could hang myself knowing what I know, and she'd be relieved because that's one less person who could tell." (In fact, Smart was indicted by a grand jury for attempting, while in jail, to arrange for another inmate to have Pierce killed.)

Police outfitted Pierce with a hidden microphone to record a conversation with Smart. According to Pierce, the two had agreed that if Pierce were ever wired, she would signal Smart with a wink. "For a few minutes," Pierce said later, "I had to think to myself, 'Should I wink?' But I didn't wink, and she told all."

Played in court, the recordings made Pam Smart sound anything but a grieving young widow. Discussing the possibility that Lattime might confess to the police, Smart sketched out her defense. "That's when I'm going to be in trouble," she said. "That's when I'm going to get arrested, but I can probably get out of it because they are not going to have any proof, ya know." Pam pointed to her "professional reputation and the course that I teach" as reasons why authorities wouldn't take Lattime's word over hers. "They are going to believe me," she said.

When Smart took the stand in her own defense, she claimed that her banter with Pierce was all part of a calculated "game," and that she was really trying to conduct her own investigation into the murder. In her testimony Pam showed virtually no emotion, even when describing her discovery of Gregg's lifeless body, seeming to confirm the prosecution's depiction of her as a killer with no conscience. "Cold, calculating, manipulative, self-centered, totally unfeeling for anybody but herself," said Derry police Captain Loring Jackson, who supervised the investigation.

Pam's lawyers denounced the state's case as "toxic soup" and characterized Flynn and his cohorts as deranged "thrill killers" who had murdered Gregg Smart to eliminate him as a romantic rival. But in the end the jury of seven women and five men needed only 13 hours of deliberation to return their guilty verdict. Judge Douglas R. Gray imposed the mandatory sentence for an accomplice to first-degree murder: life in prison without parole. (As part of their plea bargain, Flynn and Randall agreed to serve at least 28 years; Lattime would serve a minimum of 18. The boys were also expected to testify against Fowler, who had pleaded not guilty.)

Pam's parents, John and Linda Wojas—who moved from Miami to New Hampshire when she was in the eighth grade to protect her and her two siblings from the violence of big-city living—were stunned by the charges. "We try to think back through all her childhood years, if we could ever see a mean streak in her," said Pam's father, a retired airline pilot. "She was the most lovable, friendly kid."

Many who knew Pam then agree. At Derry's Pinkerton Academy, she was a cheerleader, honor student, class officer; she dated the captain of the football team. If she had any faults, they were that she needed to be the center of attention and that she was, perhaps, too determined to lead a glamorous life. Gregg's mother, Judy Smart, remembers: "She used to say to me, 'I'm going to be another Barbara Walters. I don't know how I'm going to do it, but that's my goal in life.'" The closest she got was as a disc jockey at Florida State University, where she called herself the Maiden of Metal, and where she graduated in 1988.

Police maintain that Smart was driven to murder her husband by her infatuation with Flynn and by visions of a $140,000 insurance payoff (of $90,000 that was paid to Pam shortly after Gregg's death, somewhat less than half of it had been spent by the time the account was frozen at Pam's arrest). But Gregg's parents speak of less tangible motives. They describe Pam as a manipulative woman whose emotional growth had stopped at 16. They say she was devastated when Gregg began to mature. "She didn't want to see Gregg turn into a yuppie," says Judy Smart. "She wanted him to keep his hair long, to party on weekends with their friends. But Gregg had gotten past that point. He wasn't this rock star she was talking about all the time."

Prosecutors and police investigators expressed satisfaction that out of the tawdry mess had come some measure of justice. "I think life in prison without the possibility of parole for this young lady is very fitting," said Captain Jackson, "I wish her a long life." □

WANDA HOLLOWAY

Shanna Harper with her mother, Wanda Holloway, behind her.

On the first Friday night in September in Channelview, Texas, most local teenagers—not to mention hordes of parents—head for the stadium at Channelview High to root for their beloved football team, the Falcons. Around here, football and all its panoply stir mighty passions. Before the start of a game, the crowd of several hundred rises for the invocation, which ends with a fervent prayer: "God protect our players and the cheerleaders."

These days that is no idle plea. Recently a county court convicted Wanda Holloway, 37, of plotting the contract murder of Verna Heath, 38, and even heard testimony that she had wanted to rub out Verna's 14-year-old daughter, Amber, as well. Her reason? It seems Wanda Holloway wanted Verna and Amber eliminated so that her own daughter, Shanna, 14, could win a spot on the cheerleading squad.

The Heaths and the Holloways were neighbors in the blue-collar Houston suburb of oilworkers and longshoremen. Amber and Shanna had even attended the same Christian elementary school. At one time, when the girls were younger and played together occasionally, the two mothers had been on friendly terms, meeting to go shopping or to take the kids to the local swimming pool. All that changed, though, once Amber and Shanna started competing to be cheerleaders.

In the spring of 1989, Verna got special permission from Channelview school officials for Amber, who was then in the sixth grade and still attending a Christian academy, to try out as a cheerleader at Alice Johnson Junior High School, where she planned to enroll the following fall. When Amber was elected to the team by a student vote and Shanna was not, Wanda was furious, especially since she had transferred her daughter to the public school earlier in the year so that she would be eligible.

Undeterred, Wanda tried the following year to help Shanna win a spot on the squad by supplying her with pencils and rulers bearing her name, which Shanna was supposed to hand out to schoolmates while campaigning for votes. Verna called for a closed-door meeting of the school board, and Shanna was subsequently disqualified from the tryouts for violating rules forbidding electioneering. Adding to the humiliation, Wanda said at her trial, Amber allegedly taunted Shanna in the hallways over her failure to make the squad.

After that, family and friends agree, Wanda was a woman possessed. As she saw it, Amber and Verna had conspired to thwart Shanna. "That's all she ever talked about, that cheerleading stuff," said her former father-in-law, R.E. Harper, who runs a convenience store in Channelview. "She'd go on and on about it to anybody who'd listen."

Wanda was raised in Channelview, where her father was a tester at a cement plant; her mother worked in the cafeteria at Channelview High. After graduating from high school in 1972, Wanda married a fellow Channelview student, Tony Harper, then 19, with whom she had two children, Shane, 18, and a freshman at Baylor University, and Shanna. She divorced Tony in 1980 and married Gordon Englehart, a prosperous businessman in Beaumont, Texas, who was at least 20 years her senior. That marriage lasted less than two years. Wanda returned to Channelview and began serving as an organist at the Missionary Baptist Church, where she met her third husband, C.D. Holloway. The congregation's choir director, he was also 20 years her senior and the owner of his own pipeline-construction company.

Wanda liked bragging to friends about how much money she had to spend on jewelry as well as on fancy clothes for herself and Shanna. Though she lived in a modest, three-bedroom tract house, she claimed that she and C.D. were worth some $2 million. Given Wanda's social ambitions and her apparent obsession with cheerleading, Shanna's failure to make the squad hit especially hard.

A year ago last September, Wanda ran into Terry Harper, 36, her former brother-in-law and a man with a long record of petty crime. As Harper testified, Wanda launched into a tirade about Verna. He jokingly told her that she should simply have her nemesis killed. Some months later, Wanda asked if he could really arrange to get rid of someone. Startled, he told her he could. Afterward, believing that Wanda was serious, Harper went to the Harris County sheriff's office and told them everything. He agreed to wear a wire and gather evidence against Holloway.

There were six taped conversations in all between Terry Harper and Wanda Holloway, both on the phone and in person. By turns anxious and determined, Wanda slowly but unmistakably confronted the possibility of hiring a hit man to kill the Heaths. She fretted about Shanna's chances of becoming a cheerleader on her third try. "This is a critical year," she told Harper plaintively. "She don't make it this year, she ain't never gonna make it." But when Harper pointed out that finding someone to kill a child—"doing" her, as he put it—might be difficult, Wanda's voice suddenly turned icy. "But, Terry, you don't know this little girl," she snapped. "If you knew her—ooh! I can't stand her. I mean she's a bitch. Makes me sick. I mean, I could knock her in the face, you know?"

Amber Heath in 1990

DAVID HAMPTON

Don't talk to David Hampton about regrets or remorse. Seven years ago, passing himself off as the son of Sidney Poitier—who has no son—Hampton, then 19, conned several prominent New Yorkers out of money and lodging. His victims included Osborn Elliott, then dean of the Columbia University Graduate School of Journalism, and John Jay Iselin, then president of New York City's public television station WNET. "I was the best thing that ever happened to them," said Hampton, a stylish figure with skin-tight fawn stretch pants and no verifiable address. "I enlivened their lives much the way Norman Mailer livens up Pat Buckley's dinner parties because the other people are boring."

The escapade cost Hampton nearly two years in jail. Publicity about the incident caught the eye of playwright John Guare, who used it as the basis for *Six Degrees of Separation*, a caustic, Tony-nominated comedy-drama about the insecurities of modern urban life.

After the show opened to critical raves in the summer of 1990, Hampton turned up in town again. He announced to the press that he was pursuing an acting career and "would rather be known for positive achievements than as a slickster in an off-Broadway play." Since then he has made more appearances in court than he has onstage.

Hampton has glib, almost plausible explanations for both old and new charges against him. In his version, his intentions have always been innocent. But he doesn't mind admitting that he yearns for the glitter. Born in Buffalo in 1964, the eldest of three children of an attorney, Hampton was, as he tells it, a precocious, talented and misunderstood child. Bouncing from one expensive prep school to another, he had but one strong desire: to get out of Buffalo. "There was no one who was glamorous or fabulous or outrageously talented there," said Hampton. "I mean, here I was, this fabulous child of 15, speaking three languages, and they didn't know how to deal with that. When I told my father I was going into the arts, we had a showdown, and he said he wouldn't support me." Hampton's father refuses to discuss his son.

Hampton was 17 when he made his first foray into New York City. The "Poitier" ruse was concocted to get him and a friend into Studio 54.

"We were swept in like we owned the place," said Hampton. "It was sort of a magical moment."

The moment was repeated often. While actor-director Gary Sinise was living in Melanie Griffith's New York City apartment, he allowed "David Poitier" to sleep on the sofa after being told the mystery guest was "a very close friend of Melanie's." Later, David Poitier told a group of Connecticut College students that he was casting the film version of the Broadway musical *Dreamgirls*, which his father was directing. The students let him crash in their dorms.

Back in Manhattan, Hampton used an address book belonging to a Connecticut College student to contact Jay and Lea Iselin. He told them he was a friend of their daughter Josie. He had been mugged, Hampton said. The Iselins put him up for the night and gave him $20. The next day

Hampton repeated the story to the Elliott family —this time bringing a male friend back to the apartment after everyone was asleep. When Inger Elliott, awakening Hampton the next morning, discovered the two in bed together, Hampton told her that the second youth was the nephew of Malcolm Forbes. Arrested later, Hampton pleaded guilty to a reduced charge of attempted burglary. He was given a suspended sentence and ordered to stay out of New York City. When he did not—and checked into Manhattan's Pierre Hotel as David Poitier—he was jailed.

After his release from prison in 1986, Hampton said he lived in Paris, London and Rome for three years, supporting himself as a bartender, factory worker and charmer. During his latest New York City sojourn, Hampton told students at New York University that *he* was the author of *Six Degrees*, then tried to cajole them into giving him a place to stay.

He has now hired attorney Richard Golub to represent him in a suit against Guare, *Six Degrees* director Bernard Gersten, Lincoln Center, where the play is running, and Random House, Guare's publisher. According to Golub, Hampton "created a theretofore nonexistent character as part and parcel of his unique personality," which even predated his 1983 arrest. That being the case, Golub claims, by "natural law," Hampton's "masquerade" becomes his exclusive property, and Guare and his producers have "wrongfully and outrageously profited" from Hampton's "imagination, creativity and life experiences." Golub is asking for $60 million. Truth may not only be stranger than fiction, it could wind up being more profitable. □

Pee-Wee Herman

Paul Reubens might have crept quietly into the night as just another alleged public-morals offender. Instead he set off a frenzy of media attention and sent his high-flying career as Pee-wee Herman plummeting.

Last July Reubens, 38, was arrested by undercover detectives on his way out of Sarasota, Florida's xxx-rated South Trail Cinema, an "adult" movie theater. Police, carrying out a routine undercover operation for morals offenses, charged that Reubens exposed himself and masturbated twice during a showing of a heterosexual porno flick called *Catalina Tiger Shark*. (The sting also yielded three other arrests.) An hour later the defendant was booked at the Sarasota County detention facility on the charge of "exposure of sexual organs." Reubens then made what may have been his second mistake of the evening: He voluntarily told detectives his stage name.

Even if he hadn't identified himself, the celebrated star of the five-year-running Saturday morning children's series *Pee-wee's Playhouse* wouldn't have remained incognito for long. An alert reporter for the *Sarasota Herald Tribune* recognized his real name on the police blotter the following day and, 48 hours later, the mortifying incident made national news.

Reubens admitted in a statement that he had been in the theater but "never exposed himself or engaged in any other improper activities." Despite the denial, Reuben's career seemed shattered. Last April CBS canceled *Pee-wee's Playhouse* after the network and the star had mutually agreed not to proceed on a sixth season. But following his arrest, the five reruns that were to have aired through August were yanked from the schedule. Disney-MGM Studios in Lake Buena Vista, Florida, suspended a two-minute video that Reubens had narrated for its backstage tour, and toy stores removed Pee-wee dolls from their shelves. Pee-wee Herman was history.

It was a painful way to sign off, though Reubens had already let go of his alter ego. In June the star's manager, Michael McClean, said that his client had burned out and sent Pee-wee "on an extended vacation." Reubens could not have anticipated this kind of hiatus. If convicted, he could face up to a year in jail and a $1,000 fine.

Newspaper columnists rallied to Reubens' defense, accusing CBS of overreacting, and such celebrity pals as Joan Rivers and Cyndi Lauper offered their support. "Whatever he may have done," said Bill Cosby, "he hasn't done that to children."

Seven years ago, speaking in character as Pee-wee (as he usually did during interviews), Reubens told the *New York Daily News* his simple goals: "Making a living, having good personal hygiene and staying out of jail." Since abandoning the squirmy guy in the silly suit, Reubens had maintained a low profile. Whatever happens next, at least one of his staunchest friends is sure Reubens won't starve. "He has so much money," says Cassandra Peterson, TV's Elvira, Mistress of the Dark, "he does not have to work again." That is fortunate; thanks to the guardians of public morality, he's going to have trouble. □

From left:
Paul Reubens around 1970,
during his college days, c. 1974,
as Pee-wee Herman.

MADONNA Last spring's outrage *du jour* from Madonna may really have been worth the fuss. Her film, a two-hour combination of concert footage and raunchy offstage scenes, *Truth or Dare: on the Road, Behind the Scenes, and in Bed with Madonna*, played like the most revealing home movie ever released by a major star. Indeed, even the preview trailer so shocked the Motion Picture Association of America—the ratings gods—that it was proclaimed too racy for G- or PG-rated audiences.

Among other juicy scenes raising a ruckus, the 32-year-old singer shows herself demonstrating oral sex techniques on a water bottle; recites an ode to flatulence; ogles two male dancers as they French-kiss; exposes her breasts; and confesses that, as a teenager, she had sex with a girlfriend. (The girlfriend, Moira McFarland, who appears in the film, stares blankly when Madonna blurts out this tidbit on camera. McFarland has since said she has no memory of the event.) In another segment, Madonna lies atop her mother's Michigan grave and speculates about "what she looks like now. Just a bunch of dust." She refers to ex-beau Warren Beatty as "pussy man."

The controversial project began when, on three days' notice, Madonna hired Alek Keshishian, 26, to film her Blond Ambition tour, beginning in Japan, in March 1990. Harvard grad Keshishian had impressed Madonna with his senior thesis, a pop opera film version of *Wuthering Heights*, which her agent had screened for her two years earlier.

Their collaboration is a startling, frank portrayal of a woman who may be more entertaining—and more temperamental, and cruder —offstage than on. The language isn't for the fainthearted: Watching two male dancers kiss, Madonna yelps, "Oh, God! I'm getting a hard-on!" Sitting backstage and picking petals off a daisy, she muses, "He loves me. He loves me not. He just wants to ---- me." In bed with her troupe of male dancers, she asks, "Do we want to be accepted by Hollywood?"

"No!" they chorus.

"Do we care what people think of us?" she prompts.

"No!" they reply.

"Do we want people to kiss our ass?"

"Yes!" they yell.

What may have been the most revealing scene, ironically, is surprising not for its lewdness but for its intimacy. As the camera watches, Madonna, feeling under the weather, is examined by a throat specialist in her New York City apartment. Warren Beatty, off to the side, mutters about "the insanity of doing all this on film, this insane atmosphere." When the doctor asks if Madonna wants to talk off-camera, Beatty snaps, "She doesn't want to *live* off-camera! What point is there to existing?" □

Like a virgin one minute, like a Marilyn the next, she is catholic in her excesses and unrepentant in her provocations. Oscar Wilde once said, "Wickedness is a myth invented by good people to account for the curious attractiveness of others." Madonna has no shame—and the whole world can't stop watching.

AXL ROSE The most anticipated happening of the summer was the launch of Guns N' Roses' double album and four-continent world tour. "Happening" may have been throwing roses at it.

During a July rock show in Maryland Heights, Missouri, lead singer Axl Rose became offended when local security guards, he said, ignored an unruly biker gang. After spotting one of the bikers with a video camera —forbidden at his concerts—he took matters into his own hands. Jumping off the stage, he landed on top of the camera-toting fan. Bodyguards had to hoist him back.

It was common behavior for Guns N' Roses, and the fans loved it—until the hard-rock group stalked offstage and headed for their hotel, leaving 20,000 of them waiting for the stars to finish the show. When roadies began packing up equipment, the audience went wild, pelting the stage with bottles, cans, rocks and garbage. Hundreds of seats in the brand-new amphitheater were yanked out. Speakers, huge video screens and sound equipment were trashed or stolen. Security guards tried to turn fire hoses on the mob, but the crowd seized the hoses and fired back. When 500 nightstick-wielding police arrived, they weren't exactly delicate. "Did we smack some people?" asked Major Thomas O'Connor of Maryland Heights. "You're damn right we did."

Two hours later at least 60 people—including more than a dozen police—were treated for injuries. There were 16 arrests and some $200,000 in property damage. Axl claimed the fault lay not with the group but with an inexperienced security staff. The police blamed Axl. He's been charged with five counts of misdemeanor assault and property damage carrying a combined penalty of up to four and a half years in jail and $4,500 in fines, and a warrant for his arrest has been issued. At least two people injured in the melee did file assault charges against Rose, the band or the promoter. (The group's lawyers are in for a busy time: The band is also being sued by its former drummer, Steve Adler, who claims its

members forced him to use heroin and then axed him from the band in March 1990 after he entered a rehabilitation program.)

Guns N' Roses' long-awaited twin albums *Use Your Illusion I* and *Use Your Illusion II* are runaway best-sellers. They were generally applauded by rock critics, despite some perfunctory demurs about the lyrics, variously described as misogynistic, world-class vulgar and unrelentingly spiteful. (Guns N' Roses never ignores a slight: There's a two-word obscenity directed to the city of St. Louis in the small print on the liner notes.) Given the albums' success, Guns N' Roses' tour is not likely to go gently into the night. The band— Axl's bail arrangements permitting —plans to be on the road for two long years. Batten down the hatches, folks. ☐

VANILLA ICE Rap star

Vanilla Ice seems to regularly ponder the question, "Why am I Vanilla Ice? Why didn't I go to college and become a lawyer?" One reason may be a debut album, *To the Extreme*, which sold 3.3 million copies in just nine weeks and a smash single, "Ice Ice Baby" (with a chorus borrowed from the David Bowie-Queen song "Under Pressure"), which became the first rap song ever to hit No. 1 on *Billboard*'s pop chart.

The 22-year-old self-created enigma says that he was a poor street kid, won three pro motocross titles, went to the same Miami high school as 2 Live Crew's Luther Campbell and nearly died after a knife fight in ritzy Coral Gables, Florida. (Others who know him tell a different story of a well-off kid named Robby Van Winkle who spent many of his teen years in Texas, won motocross titles only on the amateur circuit and drove a white IROC Camaro Z28 in high school.)

His mother, Beth Mino, a music teacher and classical pianist, tries to separate the real Ice from the snow job. "The lies were a smoke screen to protect the privacy of the family," she says. "But a lot is true. Economically, we weren't able to live in an elite part of Miami. He was raised predominantly with blacks, and he definitely was in a lot of trouble. When he was stabbed, I nearly died."

Ice tells of plans for a book that will reveal "the whole straight-up," then grudgingly dishes out some of the basic facts in advance (all confirmed by his mother). Born in Miami, he lived for several years in a tough section with his older brother and younger sister. He skated back and forth between Texas and Florida, living with friends and relatives, dropped out of school and earned cash building custom stereos.

Ice's deejay Earthquake recalls a 1987 talent show at City Lights, a mostly black Dallas night spot. "He really didn't stand out as a rapper," says Earthquake (Floyd Brown), who writes much of Ice's music. "Everybody knew him for his feet. He would demolish other dancers."

"Don't tell me I ain't from the streets," says Ice. "How else would a white guy learn to dance?"

So how come black rappers dis him? "None of it is my fault," he insists. "All I know is I'm here, and there's 11 million people that like me—most of them girls. I'm not in this for the money. All I'm worried about is the ladies and how nice everybody's treating me."

Does that include the California police? Ice was arrested in June for pulling a gun on a man who tried to sell him jewelry at 2:15 A.M. outside a supermarket in Studio City, California. If Ice is found guilty, he could face up to six months in jail and a $500 fine. □

Whose Life Is It, Anyway?

TOM SELLECK Some members of the gay community support a fairly recent phenomenon called outing—public identification of closet homosexuals. Predictably, the new tactic has caused a stir.

In July Tom Selleck, 46, filed a $20 million libel suit against the *Globe*, a supermarket tabloid, for his inclusion in a story about a gay-rights group that had plastered Manhattan with posters of celebrities emblazoned with the words ABSOLUTELY QUEER. Selleck, who has been married for four years to actress Jillie Mack and has a 2-year-old daughter, Hannah, declared, "I am singularly heterosexual." The *Globe* claimed that its article was "perfectly factual."

A month later the lawsuit was settled. Although financial terms were not disclosed, the tabloid issued an apology, saying it never intended to imply that Selleck was gay.

SANDRA BERNHARD

Hudson Hawk's Sandra Bernhard was out of sorts with *Outweek*, a now defunct gay magazine that derided her in print for hedging on questions about her sexuality and for claiming to date men. "I'm happy about people having insight into my sexuality. I just don't think it's necessary to have strangers tell me what I desire at any particular moment of the day," said Bernhard, 36, who is on record as being bisexual. "If I happen to want to be with men, I humbly apologize, but that's just a good possibility. I totally support the gay community, but I'm not going to deny my desires."

Bernhard did deride outing as "extremist, and any kind of extremism is not good. I guess they did it to me because they turned me into some kind of hero, and they felt like I let them down by saying something that was contrary to what they needed to hear to feel really secure."

HARVEY FIERSTEIN

Actor-playwright Harvey Fierstein, long a champion of gay rights, doesn't favor unauthorized public identification either. "Outing is something I would never do," said Fierstein, 37, who appeared in *In the Shadow of Love: A Teen AIDS Story*, on PBS in the fall. "There is no situation that I have ever been in where it was necessary.

"I have a problem with the outing of [certain celebrities]. I think it would be wonderful if [they] came out and admitted it—*if* they were gay—because it would help so many kids feel that they weren't bizarre. But what good does it do *anyone* to watch someone kicking and screaming that they're straight?" □

ELIZABETH GLASER

Ten years ago Elizabeth Glaser was infected with the AIDS virus through a tainted blood transfusion. Unaware, she passed it on to her daughter, Ariel, during breast-feeding and to her son, Jake, in utero. Elizabeth didn't know she had the virus until Ariel developed AIDS at age 4. For more than three years Elizabeth, now 43, and her husband, director Paul Michael Glaser, 47, a former star of the TV series *Starsky and Hutch*, kept their painful ordeal private.

"After we found out that my family was HIV-positive," says Elizabeth, "it was clear that I would have to grow as a person more than I had ever imagined in order to find a way to cope. I wanted to let America see how painful it is to be a family battling AIDS and how hard it is to deal with the isolation and discrimination that comes through ignorance."

Based on the experiences of other families with AIDS, Ari's doctor advised the Glasers to tell no one about their diagnosis. Ari's nursery school, however, would have to be alerted because she would need its permission to attend. Elizabeth and Paul decided to confide in a few friends. "For some," Elizabeth later wrote, "finding out that we had AIDS was like finding out that for years their children had been in imminent danger. Most of our friends wanted to stand beside us, but they also wanted assurances that there was no risk to their children. In May of 1986, answers were in short supply and there were no guarantees. You are told that you and your children may die. You are told that there are no answers now. And then as you are struggling not to completely fall apart, you realize that very few people are going to reach out to help or comfort you."

Determined to educate herself about AIDS as a national issue, Elizabeth met with physicians, politicians and friends to plan an assault on policymakers in Washington, D.C. Her first goal was to explain that AIDS affects children differently from adults and then to persuade legislators to make federal funds available, specifically for pediatric AIDS research.

Friends arranged a meeting between Elizabeth and the Reagans at the White House, where she appealed to the President to lead the nation on this urgent issue. Although the Reagans welcomed her warmly, their private concern had no impact on public policy. The more Elizabeth learned about the government's indifference to the issue of children with AIDS, the more determined she became to form a private foundation to raise funds for pediatric AIDS research.

Eight days after her 7th birthday, Ariel Glaser died. In 1989, just after the first anniversary of her death, the Glasers went public with their story when they learned that a tabloid was about to expose their tragedy in an unauthorized feature.

Elizabeth and writer Laura Palmer collaborated on *In the Absence of Angels*, an account of the Glaser family's struggles and triumphs. "If reading my story can help open hearts to people who are battling this disease," says Elizabeth, "then maybe other families will have an easier time."

More than nine years after contracting the AIDS virus, Elizabeth remains in stable health. Son Jake, too, is well. The Pediatric AIDS Foundation, which Elizabeth started with two close friends, Susan DeLaurentis and Susie Zeegen, may be small, but its ambitions are mighty: to raise money quickly, channel it directly into research and save lives. The foundation was formally launched in 1988 with a $500,000 dollar donation from Paul's aunt, Vera List. Disney chief Michael Eisner sits on the foundation's board along with Steven Spielberg and Kitty Dukakis, among others. Producer-philanthropist Ted Fields and his wife, Susie, have made generous contributions and opened their Santa Barbara ranch to doctors from the U.S. and abroad for a series of creative think-tank sessions to determine where funding is most urgently needed.

The foundation has made great strides in its short life, but Elizabeth and her team urgently press forward. "Fifty percent of America is better educated, but if you're living next door to the other 50 percent, it means nothing," says Elizabeth, who never loses sight of her power as a champion for families who lack her influence. "Like most people with AIDS, I feel aligned with the have-nots," she writes. "When I meet people in power, it's usually because they think I'm one of them. I look the same, but my goals are not their goals. They want a kinder and gentler America for themselves. My family needs an America that is kinder and gentler to all." □

71

THURGOOD MARSHALL

Thurgood Marshall's civil rights record would have been extraordinary even if his legal career had ended without his rising to the nation's highest bench. During his almost 24 years on the Supreme Court—he was appointed by Lyndon Johnson in 1967—he was its foremost crusader for social justice and the only Justice who had represented an accused murderer.

A 220-pound hulk of a man, Marshall delighted in tweaking his most powerful opponents. In 1970 pneumonia landed him in the hospital. When President Richard M. Nixon, eager to tilt the Court to the right, asked for a health report, Marshall insisted the final words read: "Not yet." Even as his body weakened—over the years he suffered a heart attack, bronchitis, blood clots, hearing loss and, most recently, glaucoma—he declared last year, "I have a lifetime appointment, and I intend to serve it."

In June, however, he announced he'd changed his mind, and resigned. "I'm old," he said. "I'm falling apart." At a press conference he divulged, with typical curmudgeonly gruffness, his future plans to "sit on my rear end." Four days later, President Bush nominated the conservative black federal appeals court judge Clarence Thomas to replace the retiring liberal.

Marshall began life in the Jim Crow world of Baltimore. Born on July 2, 1908, to William, a steward in the whites-only Gibson Island Club on the Chesapeake Bay, and Norma, a teacher at an all-black elementary school, Marshall learned early the ways of the segregated Southland. His father used to tell him, "Son, if anyone calls you a nigger, you not only got my permission to fight

him, you got my *orders* to fight him." Young Thurgood decided that his best offense was the law. Since the University of Maryland School of Law didn't accept blacks in 1930, he began commuting to the Howard University Law School in Washington, D.C.

In the years that followed, Marshall traveled the South as an attorney for the NAACP. Challenging segregation laws in court after court, Marshall became the target of racial hatred and was hidden in the homes of local black families. Often, says attorney Karen Hastie Williams, his godchild and former clerk, "there would be lynch

Thurgood Marshall with his sons in 1966.

mobs coming to get him, and he would have to go out the back door." Recalls friend and fellow NAACP attorney William Coleman: "In those days, Thurgood would be very 'courteous' and let you go through the door first. He has a real nitty-gritty sense of humor."

All told, Marshall won 29 of the 32 cases he argued as a lawyer before the Supreme Court, including the landmark 1954 *Brown* v. *Board of Education*, which ended "separate but equal" school systems. "Marshall was our savior," says NAACP activist Juanita Mitchell. "Every case they said couldn't be won, he won."

His former clerks recall him as a man who pushed past the law to the human plight. "What you get with Justice Marshall is an uncanny knack for seeing through all the legal doctrines and technicalities and precedents asking, 'Yes, but *is it fair?*'" says former clerk David Norrell. Marshall refused to conform to legal precedents, saying, "There are only two things I 'must' do —stay black and die."

Having forsaken the embattled high court, Marshall, 83, had a pacemaker implanted in September and has taken a seat on a more comfortable bench—his favorite living room chair. □

MORRIS DEES

Morris "Bubba" Dees Jr. is known around Mount Meigs, Alabama, for inventing a nifty chicken plucker and raising some of the fattest hogs in Montgomery County back in his high school days. But he's even better known as an unusually effective and courageous civil rights lawyer—the man who has won, in addition to dozens of other civil rights actions, three big cash judgments against white supremacist groups. For that reason, three times over the past 10 years, gunmen have been flushed from the tall grass by Bubba's heavily armed bodyguards. And he now rides his big bay gelding with a 9mm automatic stuck into his blue jeans. His third wife, Elizabeth Breen Dees, keeps a riot gun on her side of the bed.

The caution is not paranoiac. In 1983 Dees's office in downtown Montgomery was firebombed; since then, both it and Dees's 250-acre ranch have been turned into fortresses. In 1984 a white supremacist group named the Order plotted to assassinate Dees and Denver radio talk show host Alan Berg. Berg was gunned down when he returned home from a trip to the grocery. Security around Dees reached presidential proportions.

Dees, now 54, pioneered a novel legal strategy: filing suit against the leaderships of racist organizations to hold them financially accountable for the violent consequences of their hatemongering. The first victory came in 1987, when Dees's Southern Poverty Law Center (which he founded in 1970 with law partner Joe Levin) won a $7 million wrongful death suit against the United Klans of America by persuading a jury that its message of racial violence prompted two Klansmen to lynch Michael Donald, a young black man in Mobile, Alabama. Beulah Mae Donald, Michael's mother, was awarded the deed to the $250,000 Klan headquarters, and the local Klan was bankrupted.

Last year Dees won a $12.5 million judgment in a similar case against Thomas Metzger, head of the White Aryan Resistance, and his son John,

on behalf of the estate of Mulugeta Seraw, an Ethiopian immigrant in Portland, Oregon. Seraw was beaten to death by two skinheads who were, Dees showed, encouraged by Metzger's philosophy of racial violence.

Dees credits his bulldog commitment to justice to his father, Morris Seligman Dees Sr., who farmed cotton on a 125-acre spread near Mount Meigs. Morris, the eldest of his five children, got his first lesson in racial justice when he was 5 after he called a field hand a "big black nigger." His father took off his belt and whipped Bubba's butt.

"He wasn't no saint. He was just a good and decent man," says Dees. "If you'd said he was a liberal, he wouldn't know what you was talking about. He just gave black people what they didn't get most anywhere else, a modicum of respect. Just sitting with black friends of my daddy's, I began to feel their hurt, and I took it personal. I'm not a crusader. I don't represent causes. I represent people who have been hurt."

Seeing his father struggle as a tenant farmer, Bubba was always determined to own land. "When I was 5, I bought a pig for a dollar," says Dees. "I fattened it up and sold it for $12, then I bought eight or 10 more. I always had a feel for making money."

He graduated from high school with $5,000 in the bank, 50 head of cattle and 200 hogs. He and the first of his three wives, Beverly Crum, struck out that fall for the University of Alabama at Tuscaloosa. The next year a federal court ordered the university to admit a black student named Autherine Lucy. Watching her run the gauntlet of a screaming mob, Dees remembers, "made me feel sick to my stomach."

Dees enterprises continued to bring in money all through college, law school and the first years of his law practice in Montgomery. In 1966 he was named one of the Ten Outstanding Young Men of America by the U.S. Jaycees. On a business trip, he picked up Clarence Darrow's autobiography and read it in one sitting. "It changed my life," he says. "I decided to help people. I'd already made enough money." The next year he filed suit to integrate the Montgomery YMCA, and people in his hometown began calling him a "nigger lover."

In 1969, at age 34, Dees sold a mail-order book company to the Times-Mirror company for $6 million. Dees and his new law partner, Joe Levin, began taking on civil rights cases throughout the South. While working on George McGovern's 1972 presidential campaign (Dees's mail-order wizardry raised more than $24 million for McGovern from 600,000 small donors), Dees and Levin started the Southern Poverty Law Center. They used the McGovern mailing list to drum

...UNTIL JUST[ICE R]OLLS DOWN LIKE WATERS AND RIGHTE[OUSN]ESS LIKE A MIGHTY STREAM

MARTIN LUTHER KING JR

up financial support. For the first 10 years of the center's existence, Dees drew no salary. (Nor did he accept any of the proceeds from his recently published autobiography, *A Season for Justice*, leaving them for his coauthor.) He's now paid $101,100 a year as the center's executive director, commanding a staff of 40, including five full-time lawyers. All clients are represented free of charge.

The SPLC first made national headlines in 1975 when Dees represented Joan Little, a black North Carolina inmate who stabbed a white jailer with an ice pick when he tried to rape her. A jury found she acted in self-defense. The Dees team also forced the all-white Alabama State Police to hire its first black, stopped the use of federal funds in Alabama to sterilize poor women involuntarily and won a remarkable 50 out of 50 cases for clients on death row. "We ain't lost much," Dees says. "We hang in there till we win."

From the office of the new $5 million SPLC headquarters, built after the firebombing, Dees can look down at what he calls his proudest achievement, the Maya Lin–designed black-granite monument to 40 people killed in the civil rights movement. It's angled to face the Alabama state house where, in 1962, George Wallace pledged his allegiance to segregation. □

Operation Desert Storm

W hen it started in August 1990, Iraq had the fourth-largest army in the world, and the United States was said to have little stomach for war. When it was over, seven months later, Saddam Hussein's military machine was no longer an international threat. The United States had successfully led 25 other countries in the largest military alliance since the Korean War. Even those with misgivings about the fighting supported the 540,000 members of the U.S. Army, Navy, Marines and Air Force—including 30,000 women—who left their families for the Persian Gulf. At times it felt as if all America was over there with them, as we stayed glued to round-the-clock television coverage of both the air war and the 100-hour coup de grace on the ground.

The 1st Cavalry in the Saudi desert.

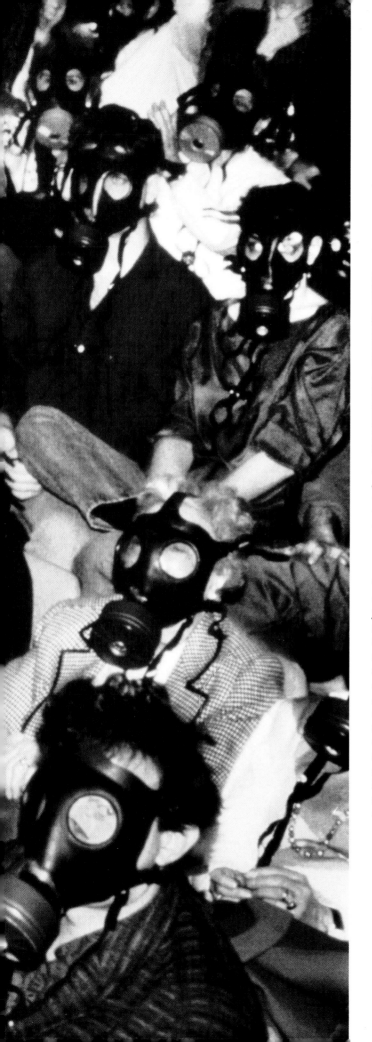

Major Marie Rossi, 32, of Oradell, New Jersey, was one of the first women to fly in a combat area. She and three members of her Chinook helicopter crew were killed in a crash on March 1.

Thirteen minutes before the February 23 deadline set by the U.S. for Iraq's withdrawal from Kuwait, sirens sounded over Jerusalem, signaling a Scud missile attack. Inside the sold-out 800-seat Sherover Theater, the ominous warning clashed with the strains of Mozart being performed by the Israel Philharmonic with renowned American violinist Isaac Stern. The orchestra left the stage, but the audience simply donned gas masks and stayed put. Moments later the 70-year-old virtuoso returned, his own mask cast aside, and for seven minutes he filled the tense concert hall with the stately notes of a Bach saraband. As he played his final note, the all-clear was given, only to be drowned out by a thunderous standing ovation.

General Schwarzkopf and his family.

General Powell with his wife and children.

"STORMIN' NORMAN"

The Iraqis were routed from Kuwait, and with the success of Operation Desert Storm came instant acclaim for the ebullient man who overwhelmed Saddam Hussein: the Commander in Chief of U.S. forces there, General H. Norman Schwarzkopf. Prior to the August 1990 invasion, Schwarzkopf, 56, was well-known, but only in Army circles. In Vietnam, where he had received two Purple Hearts and three Silver Stars, and later in Grenada, he had earned a reputation as an aggressive yet compassionate commander with an explosive temper and an intolerance for inefficiency and ineptitude. In April 1991, he came home a superstar.

After a 35-year hitch in the Army, Schwarzkopf, his mission accomplished, retired in August. He professed no deep regrets about taking off his uniform for the last time. "People have the wrong idea about generals," he said. "They think we have our stars tattooed on us."

GENERAL COLIN L. POWELL

Powell, at 54 the nation's youngest and first black Chairman of the Joint Chiefs of Staff, began his guided-missile rise through the ranks with two tours in Vietnam. He was decorated with the Bronze Star for the rescue of four buddies from a downed, burning helicopter. After a string of commands in the U.S. and Europe and a stint in the White House as national security adviser, Powell finally took his seat at the head of the Joint Chiefs' table in 1989, and soon after orchestrated the invasion of Panama to snare Manuel Noriega.

With the gulf victory behind him, Powell has expressed relief that coalition forces acted quickly to head off further Iraqi aggression. "We got enough force in there to let [Saddam Hussein] know he was pulling on Superman's cape and he better stop," he declared to a group of newspaper editors in March.

Whether he's in dress greens at a White House dinner or in fatigues mixing with the troops, the Harlem-born son of Jamaican immigrants never forgets his origins. In April he told students at Morris High School, his alma mater in the Bronx, "I remember the auditorium. I remember the feeling that you can't make it. But you can." And to an Akron, Ohio, grade-schooler who asked him about his life for Black History Month, Powell wrote back, "I never let my being black be a problem for me—if it was a problem, it was somebody else's problem, not mine." □

DR. FRANCES CONLEY

As one of the nation's first female neurosurgeons, Dr. Frances Conley, a professor at the Stanford University School of Medicine, had an outstanding 17-year reputation as both a physician and an academician. It therefore came as a shock to students and faculty last June when the 51-year-old doctor announced her resignation, charging that she had endured a career-long pattern of sexual harassment from colleagues and superiors within her male-dominated profession. She was raising in public an ugly, subterranean subject that was to become a major issue of the year.

Conley was subjected to the sort of suggestive banter that its practitioners staunchly defend as humor. "I was asked to go to bed, but it was always in jest, for effect," she recalled. "Unlike what many women have experienced, it was always said with four or five people around. The men wanted to see if I would put up with the rules of the club—a club that had always allowed men to use women as they wanted to. It was not harmful physically, but mentally it was disgusting. Often when something offensive would happen, I would talk to people about it, and the advice was always, 'Don't worry about it. That's just the way men are.'"

Over the years, Conley never formally complained about how she was treated. Her differences of opinion with male colleagues were routinely put down by them to premenstrual syndrome or being "on the rag." In an examining room Conley would be summoned to a male doctor's side with, "Hi, Hon, can you come here for a minute?" Despite her anger, Conley paid heed to the advice she had been given. "You don't make an issue out of it," she said. "You don't tell them, 'That's disgusting.' I never did. But I would today."

So perhaps will others. In October, the whole country watched as a reserved young woman, a professor of commercial law at the University of Oklahoma, testified in a riveting, nationally televised Senate hearing. Anita Hill, 35, elevated the understanding of sexual harassment, regardless of whether the truth of her charges against then Supreme Court nominee Clarence Thomas is ever conclusively resolved.

Conley saw similarities between her decision to go public and Hill's speaking out. "If we're ever going to change things," she said, "we're going to have to make sure that people in leadership positions understand the issues. Women across this country understand why Anita Hill stayed at her job, why she kept phoning Thomas. They understand you need to put up with harassment, that this is your job and your life."

Although Conley remained somewhat pessimistic about the effect of coming forward, her move sparked a nationwide discussion about sexism in the workplace and led Stanford's medical school to rethink its policies. At the urging of colleagues, Conley rejoined the faculty in September because, she said, "I felt I could do more from the inside than out." Yet her own advice to women handling sexism remained cautious. "Over the years, when women came to me for advice, I said, 'Look before you make an issue of it. Do some risk-benefit analysis, because you could still derail your career.' I think that women still have to think carefully." □

AUNG SAN SUU KYI

When Burmese opposition leader Aung San Suu Kyi won the Nobel Peace Prize in October, the world was uncertain whether she even knew of the honor. Since July 1989, the 46-year-old dissident—whose name means "A Bright Collection of Strange Victories"—has been kept under house arrest in Rangoon by the oppressive military regime she seeks to abolish.

The Nobel committee cited Suu's nonviolent quest for democracy as "one of the most extraordinary [recent] examples of civil courage in Asia." Suu carries on the struggle of her father, Aung San, who was killed by a political rival in 1947, just before Burma gained the independence from Britain that he had helped engineer.

An Oxford graduate, Suu remained outside the political fray for many years, living in England with husband Michael Aris, a British professor of Tibetan studies, and their two sons. Returning to Burma in 1988 to nurse her dying mother, Suu joined the growing protest movement, stirring crowds with her inspiring oratory until she was arrested for criticizing military leader Ne Win.

In Rangoon, Suu's neighbors used to hear her playing the piano; when the music stopped last year, some concluded she had sold the instrument to buy food. Currently a visiting professor at Harvard, Aris, who has not seen his wife since Christmas 1989, said, "The joy and pride which I and our children feel at this moment is marked by sadness and continuing apprehension."

The military rulers have said Suu may leave Burma quietly; she refuses unless they abdicate power and let her make a public speech. Unheard and unseen, she remains a powerful symbol. Last June a birthday card for her was signed by more than 1,000 people around the world. Its message:

Like the candles
On this birthday cake
The bars of repression
Will one day burn down
And set free your dream of democracy: □

BORIS YELTSIN

Boris Yeltsin may be the most popular man in the Soviet Union. As President of the Russian Republic, he is the first freely elected leader in his country's 1,000-year history. And for millions of hopeful Russians, he is the living symbol of the victory of their fledgling democracy.

When conservative hard-liners attempted to overthrow Mikhail Gorbachev and sent tanks

Boris Yeltsin, Washington, D.C., 1991.

Later he warned of "clouds of terror and dictatorship gathering over the country."

Although rumors swirled that tanks were advancing, tens of thousands of Muscovites responded to Yeltsin's appeal to defend the parliament building known as the White House. They built barricades and formed a human chain across the bridge spanning the Moscow River. And in the end, it was Yeltsin's impromptu army of ordinary Russian citizens that won the day.

Yeltsin's immense popularity predates the coup and stems from his image as an earthy Everyman. Born to a poor family in the Siberian village of Butko, young Boris had a joyless childhood amid drab surroundings. He lived with his parents, Klavdia and Nikolai, and his brother and sister in a single room in a communal hut. As a youngster he lost two fingers on his left hand when a World War II grenade detonated while he was playing with it. The injury prevented him from serving in the military, and he graduated from Ural Polytechnic Institute with a degree in civil engineering. He worked his way up through the Communist Party hierarchy, eventually becoming head of construction in Sverdlovsk, the Soviet Union's major iron- and steel-producing region. In that job he caught the attention of party leaders, who appointed him to a post on the Central Committee in 1985.

Yeltsin, 60, resigned from the Communist Party in 1990 and made his national reputation by stressing the need for instant capitalism. His crusade put him on a collision course with Soviet President Mikhail Gorbachev, who had banished him from the Politburo in 1987. Things are different now. At a press conference held on the day he returned from his three-day captivity during the coup, Gorbachev equivocated when asked whether he or Yeltsin now held more power. "We have been bound together by the situation," he said.

That may be wishful thinking. Gorbachev did not emerge from the coup a hero. Yeltsin did. □

rolling into Moscow during an abortive three-day coup last August, a defiant Yeltsin led the resistance, declaring, "Aggression will not go forward! Only democracy will win!"

Standing atop one of the tanks, he addressed the crowd that had gathered to protect his headquarters at the mammoth Russian parliament building. With the Republic flag at his back, Yeltsin rallied his supporters. "Any army against the people will not work!" he thundered. He called for a general strike, exhorting the crowd to civil disobedience against the "putschists."

CHILD STARS

What becomes of former child stars when they outgrow their pigtails and they're no longer cute?

The lucky ones, like Elizabeth Taylor, Ron Howard and Jodie Foster, go on to establish formidable adult careers. They're identified as child actors only as an afterthought. Some, like Brandon (*The Courtship of Eddie's Father*) Cruz, Emmanuel (*Webster*) Lewis, Angela (*Make Room for Daddy, Lost in Space*) Cartwright and Marc (*Julia*) Copage, manage to go on to quieter callings. Cruz, now 29, spends most of his time surfing and skateboarding; once a week he gives acting lessons to elementary school-age children in Oxnard, California, where he lives. Emmanuel Lewis, 20, is a college student in Georgia. Cartwright, 29, owns a boutique and Copage, 29, lives on investments, part-time jobs and occasional acting roles while he tries for a recording career.

But far too many aren't lucky. Who's to blame for child stars who fall? The studio? Hollywood? The parents? Puberty? The children themselves?

"On the set you are a prince or princess, and they treat you great," remembers Keith Thibodeaux, who, as 6-year-old Richard Keith, made his debut as America's tiniest mambo king, Little Ricky, on *I Love Lucy* in 1956. But Thibodeaux, now 40 and a Christian rock musician living in Jackson, Mississippi, learned that young Hollywood princes can easily turn into frogs. His subsequent noncareer embraced a spectrum of drugs from marijuana to LSD.

Paul Petersen, who played Jeff on *The Donna Reed Show* in the '50s and '60s, used drugs for about 10 years after his career ended. Last year he founded A Minor Consideration, a support group of grown child actors. Petersen, 46, is bitter about his own experiences and resents his parents for getting him into show business. "My father was a successful engineer," he told *Premiere* magazine. "We didn't need the money I made. If you ask me why I did it, the short answer is: My mother was a lot bigger than me. Parents who put their kids in show business are basically pimps," he said. "They've sold their children into showbiz."

Anissa Jones, the wide-eyed moppet who played Buffy on *Family Affair* from 1966 through 1971, never finished growing up. She died in 1976 at 18 of a massive overdose of cocaine, Quaaludes and barbiturates. Her costar, Johnnie "Jody" Whitaker, now has an import-export business in Portugal. Rusty Hamer, Danny Thomas's son on *Make Room for Daddy* from the mid 1950s to the mid '60s, left Hollywood four years after the series ended. He held odd jobs and suffered from depression and alcoholism. In 1990, at age 42, he fatally shot himself in the head. Mackenzie Phillips, 31, who was fired from *One Day at a Time* when her drug habit got out of hand—she apparently spent $300,000 on cocaine in a year—now sings with her dad, the Mamas and the Papas' John Phillips, in a new version of the band.

Billy Gray played Bud on *Father Knows Best* (1954–63). He quit show business soon after the show. "I didn't want to work; no one wanted to hire me," says Gray, who now at 54 races mo-torcycles. Elinor Donahue, 54, who played his sister, is currently on Fox's *Get a Life*; his other costar, Lauren Chapin, didn't fare so well: She fought a heroin habit, psychosis and poverty. Today, at age 45, the divorced mother of two lives in Orlando and is an evangelist and rock-band manager.

Some enjoy a gratifying second act; many more don't. □

JODIE FOSTER

JODIE FOSTER She began working at age 3, but credits her mother for protecting her from the pitfalls of Hollywood child stardom. "My mother . . . didn't want me to make hoopla comedies where I would wear pigtails and tutus," Foster recently told an interviewer. "She wanted me to be taken seriously, and to be a moral person, and looked up to as somebody who stood for the right things. And when I did *Taxi Driver*, it's not as if she didn't know who Martin Scorsese was —she dragged me to see *Mean Streets* four times."

Foster earned her first Oscar nomination at 14; in 1989 she won Best Actress honors for her portrayal of a rape victim in *The Accused*. This year the 28-year-old Yale graduate directed her first movie, *Little Man Tate*, to wide critical acclaim. □

Jodie Foster, Taxi Driver, *1975; 1991.*

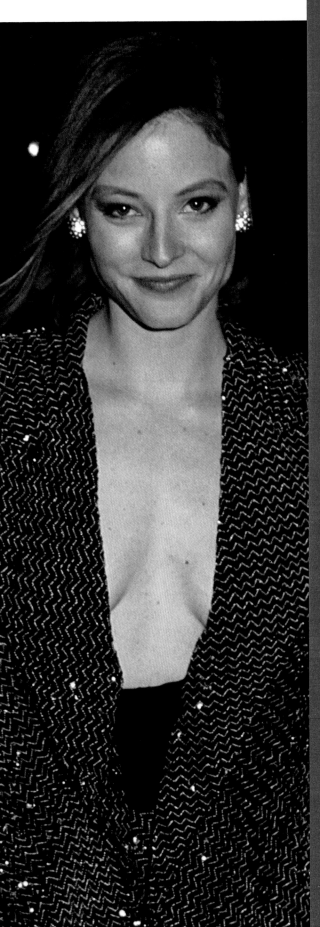

DANA PLATO During the last year, Dana Plato lost low-paying countergirl jobs at two Las Vegas dry cleaners and spent much of her time trying to win a nickel-slot jackpot at the Lakes Lounge, a neighborhood bar near the apartment she shared with her warehouse-worker boyfriend and another roommate. In February, on the day before her rent was due, Plato, 26, applied for a $6-an-hour job picking up garbage and cleaning bathrooms at her building but was turned down. Desperate, she put on a black hat and black wraparound sunglasses and, brandishing a pellet gun, robbed a local video store of $164. As Plato fled, the clerk called 911. "I've just been robbed by the girl who played Kimberly on *Diff'rent Strokes*," she said. When Plato inexplicably returned to the scene 15 minutes later, she was immediately arrested and charged with armed robbery.

Plato started acting in TV commercials at age 6 and won her *Strokes* role at 12. Six years later a pregnancy forced her to leave the show. She married the baby's father, but separated from him within a year. Meanwhile, Plato's estranged adoptive father, Dean, unsuccessfully sued her for support, and then her mother, with whom she was close, died of a blood disease. After four years, unable to make ends meet, Plato voluntarily turned her son, Tyler, over to his father. Constantly trying to revive her career, Plato even posed nude for *Playboy* in 1989. Nothing worked.

Todd Bridges, Charlotte Rae, Gary Coleman, Dana Plato, Conrad Bain, 1979.

Dana Plato

Plato's crime made instant headlines, prompting some speculation that the robbery was a publicity stunt. At the very least, it drew fresh attention to the tribulations of her beleaguered fellow *Strokes*' cast members. Todd Bridges, 25, was acquitted of murder and manslaughter (he had been charged with shooting an accused drug dealer in a crack house) in August 1990 and has a police record that goes back to 1983. Gary Coleman, 23, the diminutive 4'8" actor who was an '80s TV phenomenon, has been surviving by using a portable self-dialysis machine since his second kidney transplant failed five years ago; he is suing his parents over the handling of his $18 million fortune.

Comedian Jay Leno quipped in a *Tonight Show* monologue that the *Strokes* cast would do a reunion show "on *America's Most Wanted*." But it was no joke to those involved. Plato was given a six-year suspended sentence and will be on probation for five years. Bridges, who lives outside Los Angeles and says he is now drug free, is trying to jump-start his career. Coleman has reportedly been hospitalized at least twice (his agent says Coleman is sometimes lax with his dialysis treatments) and spends time in Tucson, Denver and Los Angeles, putting in hours each day on his hobby, collecting model trains. Adult roles that suit his stature have been hard to come by. □

Todd Bridges

Gary Coleman

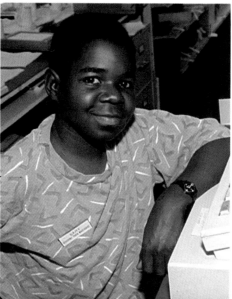

DANNY BONADUCE

After *The Partridge Family* was canceled in 1974, Danny Bonaduce's career and his personal life took a plunge. By age 21 he had squandered all of his $350,000 in savings, and in 1985 he was arrested in Hollywood for possession of cocaine. Last year it was drugs, again. Police in Daytona, Florida, were staking out a public housing project when they saw Bonaduce arrive at 2 A.M. and allegedly purchase about $20 worth of crack-cocaine. This year Bonaduce pleaded guilty to reduced charges stemming from his assault on a transvestite prostitute in Phoenix.

Most recently, a cleaned-up Bonaduce was reunited with former *Partridge* costar David Cassidy at Manhattan's Bottom Line. Bonaduce, a onetime radio disc jockey, did stand-up comedy and Cassidy—also trying for a comeback—rocked out. □

Clockwise, from top left: Susan Dey, David Cassidy, Danny Bonaduce, Suzanne Crough, Shirley Jones, Jeremy Gelbwaks, 1970.

Danny Bonaduce

Adam Rich

Adam Rich, Dick Van Patten, 1978.

ADAM RICH

He was a particularly likable moppet, invariably described as "cute little Nicholas" during the four seasons he played the youngest child on the popular series *Eight Is Enough*. But at 11 Adam Rich was drinking, at 12 he was smoking pot, and by 19 he was snorting cocaine.

Rich, now 22, was arrested in April for suspicion of breaking into a West Hills pharmacy in suburban Los Angeles. Prosecutors said that Rich, who allegedly smashed through a window with a tire iron, wanted to steal morphine, and that minutes before the break-in he had been at the nearby Humana Hospital emergency room, where he requested (and was denied) medication to dull pain in his right shoulder.

When he was arrested, Rich contacted his TV dad, Dick Van Patten. Van Patten, himself a former child star—he played Nels on TV's *I Remember Mama* from 1949 to 1956—has had a soft spot for Rich from the time he joined the show in 1977. Van Patten immediately posted the $5,000 bail. Barely 24 hours later, Rich bailed himself out for $250 after he was arrested for shoplifting sunglasses and socks from a department store. Afterward, he checked into the Betty Ford Center for five weeks. It was his second visit to the treatment facility—the first, for cocaine addiction, was in 1989—and his fifth attempt to overcome a drug-and-alcohol problem that, he ruefully estimates, has cost him a million dollars over a decade.

After getting out of the Betty Ford Center, Rich went into a recovery facility in Santa Monica, where he attended daily support meetings. Sadly, this latest attempt to overcome his problems didn't do the trick; in October Rich was once again arrested, for allegedly taking a hypodermic believed to contain Demerol from a hospital where he was being treated for a dislocated shoulder. □

SANDRA DEE

Look at me, I'm Sandra Dee
Lousy with virginity
Won't go to bed till I'm legally wed—
I can't; I'm Sandra Dee.
—from the musical, Grease, 1978.

She wasn't sultry or even particularly sexy, but when it came to budding femininity and an appealing, doe-eyed vulnerability, no actress, past or present, could ever compete with Sandra Dee. During the late 1950s and early '60s, Dee was the teen ideal, Hollywood-style—saucy yet virginal, vivacious yet demure. Years after she had disappeared from view, her image as the golden teen who all but defined the decade was nostalgically resurrected in the musical, *Grease.*

Dee was a successful model from the time she was 10; later she parlayed her nubile poutiness and the sweetest smile on the beach into stardom in romantic comedies like *Gidget* and *Tammy Tell Me True*, as well as in the melodramas *Imitation of Life* and *A Summer Place.* In 1960, when she was 18, she eloped with crooner Bobby Darin, 24, whose own career was soaring, thanks to hits such as "Mack the Knife" and "Splish Splash." In the pages of the fan magazines it read like a storybook life.

The reality was nothing that the America of that time could imagine or that Hollywood would have wanted to know. As a child, she was sexually abused by a domineering stepfather 40 years older than her mother. "He used to say, 'I'm not marrying your mother. I'm marrying both of you,'" Dee recalled. "While my mother was dating him, he began fondling me." After her mother married, things became worse. Dee accompanied them on their honeymoon, and in the hotel, they all got in bed together. "He had me sleep in the middle," said Dee. "That became the routine. My dad got me to have sex with him. I didn't understand what was going on. I was a child. By the time I was 11, I knew it wasn't right. But what could I do, tell my mother? I figured she knew." Overbearing, possessive and self-protective, her mother never acknowledged the abuse—and even added to Dee's self-loathing by encouraging her daughter to bind her prematurely developed breasts to keep her looking childlike.

Later, although her marriage to Darin was basically a happy one, she says, "It ended with a suddenness I still can't explain. But Bobby had a cold streak in him. He could turn you off like a light switch." Dee drank heavily following her 1967 divorce and more heavily still after Darin's death, at 37, in 1973. Her shame led to a decades-long plunge into anorexia, drug-and-alcohol addiction—and her eventual disappearance from the public eye.

In 1988, when her mother died, Dee hit bottom and was eventually hospitalized. With the help of a psychotherapist and the love and support of her son, Dodd Darin, 29, the former teen queen is finally shaking free of her past. Recently she made her first acting appearance in 10 years in *Love Letters*, a play, in Los Angeles. □

Clockwise, from left: Sandra Dee, 1958; 1991; with husband Bobby Darin, 1961.

Michael (right, foreground), the rest of the Jackson 5 and their parents.

MICHAEL JACKSON

When the Jackson 5 began performing together in 1963, 5-year-old Michael was notable mostly for his appealing energy and dancing ability. But his performing genius eventually made him unofficial group leader, and ultimately his talents as a solo artist and songwriter overshadowed the achievements of his brothers. His sister Janet, 24, is the only other Jackson sibling—there are nine of them altogether—who has had notable solo success.

As a result, Michael's relationship with family members has occasionally been strained, but his generosity toward friends, acquaintances and children is legend. And while some may wonder about a grown superstar who lives in a place called the Neverland Ranch (complete with a private amusement park, a zoo, a chimpanzee named Bubbles and his very own giraffe), at least Michael Jackson shares his toys. On weekends he often entertains busloads of needy or handicapped children as well as his own nieces and nephews.

If his demeanor is shy and childlike, when it comes to business he knows how to play with the big boys. This year, at 32, Michael Jackson moon-walked into the biggest deal in music history. Sony, the Japanese giant that ate CBS Records in 1988, signed him to a six-album record and film contract that some of those involved claimed might earn him as much as $1 billion. While that number

appeared to rest on deeply suspect assumptions—for example, that the new *Dangerous* and subsequent records would continue to sell as briskly as *Thriller* (which, at 40 million copies, is the best-selling LP of all time)—the deal did set new standards for cost and scope. Jackson got the highest record royalty rate in music—25 percent of every album sold—and was made CEO of his own Nation Records label. Furthermore, he heads up a new Jackson Entertainment Complex to oversee production of Jackson-related films, TV projects and music videos.

Some Jackson watchers speculated that Michael timed the announcement of his Sony contract to upstage sister Janet. One week earlier she had signed what was—for several days—the most lucrative contract in music, an estimated $50 million, three-album deal with Virgin Records.

Jackson rarely talks about himself, his family or his childhood, offering few clues to the real Michael other than what's there for the world to see. But when New York *Newsday* columnist Liz Smith asked him about the opulent wedding he hosted for friend Elizabeth Taylor (most of which Jackson paid for), he said, "I would do anything for Elizabeth. I truly love her. We're so much alike, you know. She and I, we're exactly alike. It's hard being a child star and having to grow up, but she and I understand each other and all about it." □

JOSEPH PAPP changed the face of American theater and lived a life nearly as tempestuous as anything he ever brought to the stage. Charismatic and controversial, the exuberant impresario who founded the New York Shakespeare Festival and helped create such classics as *A Chorus Line* embraced long shots and scoffed at the establishment. In the course of producing more than 350 plays, he uncovered an astonishing trove of new talent. It was Papp who promoted playwrights David Mamet, John Guare and David Rabe and who championed young actors including George C. Scott, Colleen Dewhurst and Meryl Streep. After his death from prostate cancer at 70, Papp was mourned not only by his wife of 15 years, Gail Merrifield, four surviving children, three grandchildren and three ex-wives, but also by a generation of theatergoers.

As the second of four children of Eastern European immigrants, the Brooklyn-born Yosl Papirofsky endured a family life marked by violence and deprivation.

Not until the Yiddish-speaking Yosl was old enough to go to school did he learn English; at 12, when he went into the local public library and discovered the works of Shakespeare, his life was changed forever. After serving in the Army during World War II—where he staged armed-services variety shows whose stars included Bob Fosse—Papp studied acting and directing on the GI Bill. Using sheer nerve and his skimpy savings, he mounted bare-bones but ambitious productions. In 1957 he took his troupe on the road, where they performed on a flatbed truck. His dream was to do Shakespeare free and outdoors.

When his truck broke down in Central Park, he stayed there, and with funds that he helped pull together, the Delacorte Theater was completed in 1962. Four years later Papp prevailed upon the city to turn over the Astor Library as headquarters for the Public Theater. There, during the following decades, he staged such groundbreaking plays as *Hair* and *The Normal Heart*. He battled with critics, fostered minority playwrights like Ntozake Shange and

persuaded Linda Ronstadt to do Gilbert and Sullivan. With choreographer Michael Bennett, Papp developed *A Chorus Line* and used its gusher of proceeds to fuel his work at the Public. Overall, the plays that Papp produced collected three Pulitzer prizes, 28 Tonys and more than 90 Obies.

A voracious intellectual who reminded one writer of "a Renaissance scholar on Benzedrine," Papp was slowed down by a five-year struggle against cancer and the death of his only son, Tony, who died of AIDS at 29 in June. □

David Lean

DAVID LEAN, the virtuoso British filmmaker who directed such classics as *Brief Encounter* (1945), *Great Expectations* (1946), *The Bridge on the River Kwai* (1957), *Lawrence of Arabia* (1962), *Doctor Zhivago* (1965) and *A Passage to India* (1984), died at 83 after a long illness in London. Lean, who got into the business at 19 by fetching tea at a British studio, made 16 films during his 49-year career. They collected a total of 28 Oscars, and Lean himself was named Best Director twice. □

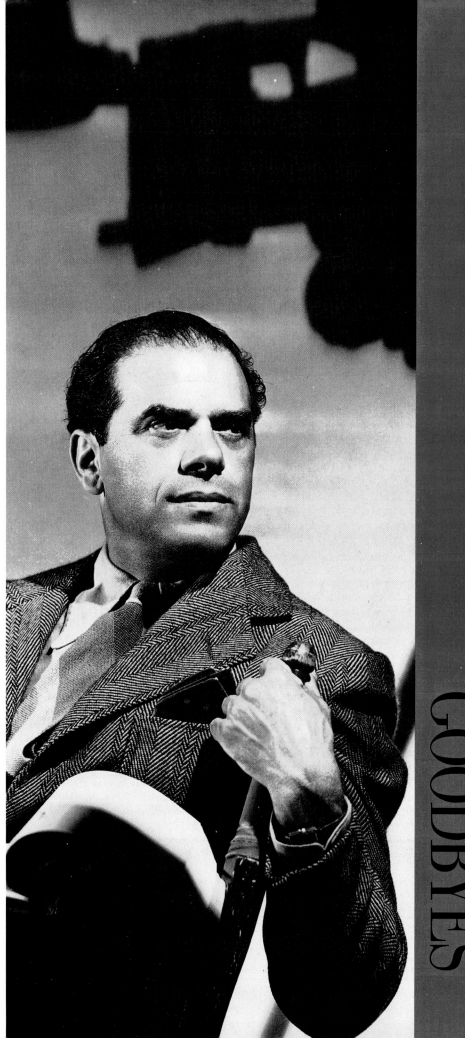

Frank Capra, late 1940s.

FRANK CAPRA

Director Frank Capra saw American life as an epic struggle between the decent guys and the rest, and in Capra's unrepentantly sentimental world, the decent guys always won.

Capra served up his version of the American dream in more than twoscore films over four decades. In the process, he won three Oscars for directing (*It Happened One Night*, 1934; *Mr. Deeds Goes to Town*, 1936; and *You Can't Take It with You*, 1938) and became one of the first Hollywood directors to see his name bannered above the film title in the credits.

When he died peacefully in his sleep at his home in La Quinta, California, the 94-year-old Capra left behind a legacy that endeared him to moviegoers long after the lights had gone out on his career. The youngest son of a Sicilian peasant, Capra worked his way through the California Institute of Technology and got his movie training thinking up gags for Mack Sennett comedies. Steven Spielberg spoke for millions of the director's fans when he said, "Frank Capra made old-fashioned American values—and crying in the movies—a national pastime."

But after World War II, during which he made the inspirational *Why We Fight* films, Capra's star declined. His Depression-era sentimentality seemed hopelessly outdated; even *It's a Wonderful Life* was all but buried until resurrected by TV as the American *Christmas Carol*. Although he fought against the rising power of film superstars, in 1961 he abandoned his own creed ("Never plead. Always have your hat on, ready to walk out") and virtually surrendered control of *Pocketful of Miracles* to an overweening Glenn Ford. The disillusioned Capra never made another picture.

Until he suffered a series of minor strokes, Capra toured college campuses, criticizing Hollywood's lack of originality and urging students to pursue their own creative vision. As he put it, "Only the morally courageous are worthy of speaking to their fellow man for two hours in the dark." □

They divorced in 1965, remarried—and divorced for good in 1972. "I always said we got on much better during the divorces," Dewhurst later reflected. "We make a better brother and sister."

Her blood brother onstage was Jason Robards Jr. Together they carved the definitive modern renditions of Eugene O'Neill, first in the 1973 revival of *A Moon for the Misbegotten*, for which Dewhurst won a Tony, and later in *Ah, Wilderness!* and *Long Day's Journey into Night*.

Dewhurst was a relentless crusader. For the past six years she served as president of Actors' Equity, fighting to support actors with AIDS and, unsuccessfully, to save Broadway's Morosco and Helen Hayes theaters from developers. Several years ago she said of her life: "God knows I've made mistakes, some of them close to tragedies, but then I suppose I'm greedy. I wanted it all." □

COLLEEN DEWHURST

created many memorable moments in her four decades as a stage and screen actress. But curiously enough, one of the most poignant came when she appeared as Candice Bergen's overbearing mother on CBS's *Murphy Brown*. In one episode, after her mother has ridden roughshod over her for a solid 20 minutes, Murphy is awakened late at night by the scratch and wail of an old phonograph record. Sneaking out to the living room, she catches her mother recapturing her lost youth: swaying about the room to a Billie Holiday record, a rose clenched in her teeth.

That performance, for which she won her third Emmy, was vintage Dewhurst. With her full, chiseled features and a voice like a steel file on granite, Dewhurst, who died of cancer at 67, embodied every modern woman trying to claw a place for herself in a world run by men. Yet she also had a downy sweetness about her.

"She's like an Earth Mother," her friend Maureen Stapleton once said, "but in real life she's not to be let out without a keeper. She's a pushover, a pussycat. She's the madonna of the birds with broken wings."

The combination helped make her one of America's most formidable, and most beloved, actresses. Canadian-born, Dewhurst went to New York City in 1946. There she waited on tables and answered phones while studying at the American Academy of Dramatic Arts. Despite her claim that she wasn't raised to be married, she wed a fellow student and spent 10 years doing bit parts and summer stock. Eventually she caught the eye of theater impresario Joseph Papp, who offered her the role of Kate in *Taming of the Shrew*. Two years later, in 1958, she appeared in José Quintero's *Children of Darkness* with another struggling actor, George C. Scott. In less than two years they had divorced their spouses and married.

It proved a volatile union even by show business standards. They had two sons (Alexander, 31, a stage manager and playwright, and Campbell, 30, with whom Dewhurst appeared in the recent Julia Roberts vehicle *Dying Young*).

JOAN CAULFIELD,

a wide-eyed blond beauty who played wholesome ingenues in light films in the 1940s, died at 65 of cancer in Los Angeles. She also starred in such early TV series as *My Favorite Husband*, which ran from 1953 to 1955, and *Sally*, from 1957 to 1958. □

MILDRED DUNNOCK

Actress Mildred Dunnock, who played Willy Loman's stoic wife, Linda, in the original stage, movie and TV versions of *Death of a Salesman*, died at 90 of natural causes on Martha's Vineyard, Massachusetts. She also appeared in 23 films, including *Love Me Tender* with Elvis Presley and *Butterfield 8* with Elizabeth Taylor. □

NATALIE SCHAFER,

who played Lovey, the daffy wife of millionaire Thurston Howell III on the popular '60s sitcom *Gilligan's Island*, died at 90 of cancer in Beverly Hills. "We never knew how old she was," said Bob Denver, who played Gilligan. "Every time she was asked her age, she'd reply, 'What was it last year?'" □

Jean Arthur

JEAN ARTHUR, the street-
smart blond with the husky voice
and innocent eyes, died at 90 of
heart failure in Carmel, California. Born Gladys Georgianna
Greene in the Bronx, Arthur, who
named herself for Jeanne D'Arc
and King Arthur, achieved fame
in Frank Capra's *Mr. Deeds Goes
to Town* (opposite Gary Cooper)
and *Mr. Smith Goes to Washington*
(with Jimmy Stewart). A recluse
offscreen, she left Hollywood in
1953 after filming *Shane*, only to
return 13 years later for one short-
lived TV series, *The Jean Arthur
Show*. Twice married and divorced, she briefly taught acting at
Vassar before retiring for good to
her Big Sur estate, Driftwood. □

EVA LE GALLIENNE
Actress-producer Eva Le
Gallienne, one of the last remain-
ing grandes dames of American
theater, died of heart failure at
92 in Weston, Connecticut.
Le Gallienne, who was born in
London, made her stage debut
there in 1914. She came to the
U.S. a year later and quickly became one of Broadway's leading
stars. Le Gallienne started the
famed Civic Repertory Theatre in
1926, directing and starring in
many of its productions until it
folded because of the Depression.
She received an Oscar nomination in 1981 for her last film,
Resurrection. □

DAME PEGGY
ASHCROFT, the versatile
actress considered by many to be
the first lady of the English stage,
died at 83 after suffering a stroke
in London. During her 65-year
career, Ashcroft played opposite
the great leading men of her time,
ranging from Sir Laurence Oliv-
ier to Paul Robeson (with whom
she had an affair). She was familiar to American audiences most
recently for her performances in
TV's *The Jewel in the Crown* and
the film *A Passage to India.* □

Eva Le Gallienne, Hedda Gabler, *1930s.*

CORAL BROWNE, the
tart-tongued, Australian-born actress whose best film roles were in
the British movies *The Ruling
Class* (1972) and *Dreamchild*
(1985), died at 77 of breast cancer in Los Angeles. She had been
seen earlier in the year in ads for
a bug repellent with Vincent Price,
80, her husband of 17 years. □

JULIE BOVASSO, an
actress and avant-garde playwright,
died at 61 of cancer in New York
City. Bovasso, who had in recent
years specialized in playing Italian
matriarchs onscreen, portrayed
John Travolta's mother in both
Saturday Night Fever and its
sequel, *Staying Alive*. In 1987
Bovasso appeared in *Moonstruck*
and served as the movie's dialect
coach. □

Dame Peggy Ashcroft,
The Jewel in the Crown,
1984.

LEE REMICK Last April,
when friends heard that Lee
Remick had suddenly dropped
out of the musical *A Little Night
Music*, they feared her days were
numbered. In July, the elegant
actress lost her two-year battle
with kidney and lung cancer at
55. She died at her home in
Brentwood, California. By her
side were her husband of 21 years,
William "Kip" Gowans, 61, and
her children by an earlier marriage to director Bill Colleran—
writer Kate Sullivan, 32, and rock
guitarist Matthew, 30.

More than 200 friends gathered
at Westwood Mortuary to bid
Remick farewell. Jack Lemmon
and Gregory Peck delivered eulo-
gies, and her children sang the
title song from *Anyone Can Whis-
tle*, her 1964 Broadway musical.

To the end, Remick described
her life as "charmed." The daughter of Frank Remick, a wealthy
Quincy, Massachusetts, depart-
ment-store owner, and actress Pat
Packard, Lee was taken by her
mother to New York City at age 7
after her parents' 1942 divorce.
She attended the fashionable
Hewitt School and then Barnard
College, before dropping out to
pursue her dream of acting.

Remick made her debut as a
baton-twirling sexpot in *A Face in
the Crowd* in 1957, and made
her name in such films as *Anat-
omy of a Murder* (1959) and *Days
of Wine and Roses* (1962). In
recent years she thrived in TV
films and miniseries, including
Jennie, *QBVII* and *Nutcracker*.
She was nominated for an Oscar,
six Emmys and a Tony. She never
won.

An intensely private person,
Remick went public with her illness to undo its stigma. Accepting
the Cancervive 1990 Victory
Award, she noted, "Of all the performances in my life, this one
counts the most." Lee Remick
exited as she entered—with
class. □

Lee Remick, 1987.

MARGOT FONTEYN

Her mother meant her to learn to tap-dance, so at age 4 Peggy Hookham was taken along to Miss Grace Bosustow's dance school in the London suburb of Ealing. An early teacher quickly put an end to those notions.

So began the soaring legend of Dame Margot Fonteyn, the prima ballerina of Britain's Royal Ballet and for four decades a universal symbol of dance. She danced as a snowflake in *The Nutcracker* at age 14; she danced as Princess Aurora in *The Sleeping Beauty*, her most luminous role; she danced *Giselle* and *Swan Lake*; and when she danced with Rudolf Nureyev in *Romeo and Juliet* at London's Covent Garden in 1965, the pair stood onstage for 40 minutes to answer 43 curtain calls. She radiated elegance, intensity and a serene durability that made it seem as if she would dance forever.

Alas, she could not. After a 2½-year bout with cancer, Fonteyn died at 71. She left behind a trail of lyrical performances, lavish tributes and memories of flowers heaped on stages by delirious fans. British poet Sacheverell Sitwell once called her "a bird of beautiful plumage taking pleasure and exulting in its wings."

Off the stage on which she twirled and wept, Fonteyn was a woman of solidly middle-class British pieties. Her father was an English engineer; her mother, the former Hilda Fontes (which Margot anglicized to Fonteyn), was half-Irish and half-Brazilian.

Fonteyn was apprenticed at London's Vic-Wells Ballet. The harsh discipline of dance was lightened by performances at Cambridge University, where she met a young student named Roberto (Tito) Arias, son of the former President of Panama. Their romance was sundered by World War II, and she scarcely saw Tito again until 1953. By then she was an international star—and Tito was a committed left-wing political figure and the married father of three. After seeing Fonteyn onstage in New York City, however, Tito appeared at her hotel room one morning and announced, "You're

Dame Margot Fonteyn, 1950.

going to marry me and be very happy."

Eventually she did, and they were. They sailed the Mediterranean with Aristotle Onassis and hobnobbed with Winston Churchill. Back home in Panama, however, Tito was persona non grata. At one point Fonteyn was arrested and briefly detained in a Panamanian prison by an official who had been present at her wedding in Paris. She was deported to Miami, and Tito escaped to Brazil. Five years later Tito was shot by a would-be assassin in Panama City.

He survived, but the bullet left him paralyzed and all but speechless. Tirelessly, Fonteyn nursed Tito back to health, even as she continued to dance around the globe. In the Soviet Union in 1961, she heard whispers that a brilliant young dancer had defected to the West. Back in London, her former teacher proposed that Margot dance *Giselle* with the celebrated defector—Rudolf Nureyev. She was by then 42, nearly two decades Nureyev's senior, and considering retirement. As she later put it, "I thought, 'It would be like mutton dancing with lamb.'"

Fonteyn took up with the lamb nonetheless, and for 15 years she

and Nureyev electrified audiences in capitals around the world. She continued to divide her time between tours and her home in Panama, where Tito conducted business from a wheelchair. Already named Dame of the Order of the British Empire, she miraculously defied gravity until age 60. Ultimately, at a gala celebration at London's Royal Opera House, she danced a farewell performance. Then she gracefully retired to Panama with her husband and thereafter made only rare guest appearances. Tito died in 1989; the cost of his care had left Margot in such straitened circumstances that the Royal Ballet mounted a special benefit for her last year.

She will be remembered as one of the century's prima ballerinas, an artist who wed understated passion with the purity of form to place an indelible British stamp on the world of dance. She will be remembered by friends, artists and fans. Perhaps most of all, she will be remembered by four generations of little girls who strained, in tutus and satin slippers, hoping someday to dance *The Sleeping Beauty* in the sublime footsteps of Dame Margot Fonteyn. □

Arthur Murray and partner.

ARTHUR MURRAY

Ballroom dance king Arthur Murray, who taught Rockefellers, Vanderbilts and countless others less well-known to shuffle their feet to the beat, died of pneumonia in Honolulu. He was 95. Born Arthur Murray Teichman, the son of an Austrian baker in New York City, Murray had by the mid-1920s waltzed his way from life as a 15-cents-a-dance instructor to being America's preeminent dance master. Millions of Americans, footstep diagrams in hand, learned to rumba, fox-trot and bunny hug at his chain of Arthur Murray dance studios, which at its height, in 1964, numbered more than 300. (Murray had sold them for $5 million in 1952.) He is survived by his wife of 65 years, Kathryn Kohnfelder, who co-starred on his popular TV show, *The Arthur Murray Party*, which ran from 1950 to 1960. In recent decades, Murray, whose favorite dance was the bossa nova, showed little enthusiasm for rock and roll, explaining, "I don't like dancing alone, and I feel silly flailing my arms around." □

MARTHA GRAHAM

One Sunday morning shortly before the turn of the century, a Pittsburgh doctor and his wife took their 2-year-old daughter to a Presbyterian church. When the organ music started, the child broke away from her embarrassed mother and began pirouetting up the aisle.

It was fitting that the first public performance of Martha Graham was something of a shocker. She had been a rule breaker and a groundbreaker for more than six decades and she was 96 when she died of cardiac arrest in her New York City home last April. The long-faced woman with the imperial bun of black hair was to dance what Picasso was to painting and Joyce was to literature. One of the most influential dancers, choreographers and teachers of the 20th century, she revolutionized her art, ending the 350-year tyranny of classical ballet with its vaulting leaps, pointed toes and intellectual precision. Instead, Graham favored—and created—the muscular, sensual, earthbound movements of what became known as modern dance. "Out of emotion," she once said, "comes form." The results of her philosophy—"I don't want to be understandable, I want to be felt"—enchanted audiences from Toledo to Tokyo.

Graham was a diminutive woman—only 5′3″—but her stature and her stamina were enormous. During her lifetime, Graham created so many memorable works that she was lionized by the dance world in virtually every decade of her professional reign. She danced and choreographed to music as fresh and diverse as Aaron Copland's *Appalachian Spring* and Scott Joplin's *Maple Leaf Rag.* "As a dancer, when I was studying with her all those years ago, Martha helped form my body," said one of her more famous pupils, former First Lady Betty Ford. "As a woman of independent thought, she helped form my mind."

The eldest daughter of George and Jane Graham, Martha moved with her family to Santa Barbara, California, in 1908. When she was a freshman in high school, her parents took her to see the early modern dancers Ruth St. Denis and Ted Shawn in Los Angeles—and she was hooked. She spent her next three summers at their Denishawn dance school and enrolled in the company after completing junior college.

By the mid-'20s Graham was a fixture in Greenwich Village, forming her first dance company and teaching body movement to budding actors at the Neighborhood Playhouse. Among her pupils over the years: Eli Wallach, Gregory Peck, Joanne Woodward, Woody Allen, Tony Randall, Bette Davis —and, more recently, Madonna, who says she wants to play Graham if a movie is ever made of her life.

Graham was accompanied at her 1926 New York City dance debut by composer Louis Horst, who wrote original scores for several of Graham's works and was romantically involved with her for many years. They maintained a professional partnership until 1949. When Horst died 15 years later, she destroyed their entire correspondence so that no one could ever learn the extent of their relationship. In 1948 Graham married a dancer in her company, Erick Hawkins, who was 14 years her junior. The marriage lasted only two years, and they had no children.

Until Graham stopped dancing —incredibly, not until she was 75— she usually cast herself as the lead in her own creations, mainly dances with strong psychological themes. It took two years for her to adjust to not dancing. But when she returned to choreography in 1971, it was with a fury. She remained at the cutting edge of the dance world until her death and was working on a new piece about Christopher Columbus for the 500th anniversary of the discovery of America. The work would have been her 181st. "Dance is my passion," she once said. "It's all I really know." □

Martha Graham

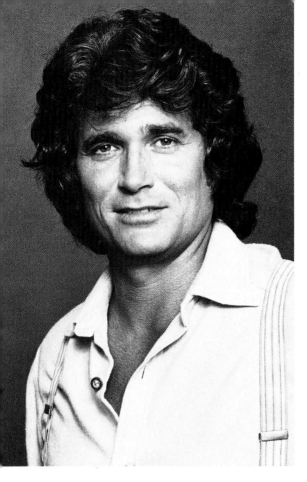

MICHAEL LANDON

After a ferocious three-month battle, Michael Landon succumbed to pancreatic cancer quietly, with the family he cherished near his bed. On his last weekend the 54-year-old gathered his inner circle at his Malibu ranch: his wife, Cindy, all nine of his children, his business partner, Kent McCray, and McCray's wife. They kept a vigil in Landon's upstairs bedroom. Very near the end, Landon asked for time with Cindy. She was the only one with him when he died.

To television viewers over the last three decades, Michael Landon, shaggy haired and ruggedly boyish, personified old-fashioned American values: love of family, neighborliness and a bulldog perseverance against all calamities, natural and man-made. As a writer, director and producer, he became phenomenally successful, one of the few actors to grab the reins of his own career and harness it to his personal vision.

Landon was a perfectionist who spent a lifetime trying to perform and portray worthy deeds and then kicking tail when anyone got in his way. This sense of solitary righteousness—and frontier methods of inflicting his will—was bred into Landon early. Born Eugene Orowitz in Forest Hills, New York, he grew up with his sister in Collingswood, New Jersey. His Jewish father, Eli Orowitz, was a theater manager and film publicist; his Irish-Catholic mother, Peggy O'Neill, was a minor actress before giving up her career. Throughout his childhood, Landon watched his parents bicker endlessly or not talk to one another for weeks. Volatile and unstable, his mother made frequent but halfhearted attempts to take her life. Years later Landon tried to exorcise childhood demons with humor. "I was 10," he would say, "before I knew you put anything but a head into a gas oven."

Outside his home, things were no better. High school boys screamed "Jew bastard!" at Landon from passing cars. In a largely Christian community, fathers wouldn't allow their daughters to go out with him. The family and social pressures made him a chronic bedwetter. The humiliation was increased by his mother's practice of hanging the soaked sheets from his bedroom window.

College only reinforced his sense of isolation. Eugene (who changed his name to Michael Lane in the '50s and finally to Michael Landon) forged himself into a top-flight javelin thrower in high school and set the national record in his senior year. That won him a track scholarship to the University of Southern California. His teammates took exception to his shaggy locks and even pinned him down and cut off his hair. Landon, furious, threw his arm out on a toss. The damage eventually cost him his scholarship and he soon quit school.

It would seem that virtually all Landon's experiences as a youth were harsh ones: In 1954 he accompanied his publicity-agent father to Los Angeles because the older man believed that his former colleagues at RKO Radio Pictures, by now at Paramount studios, would offer him a job. None of the executives he asked for remembered him. He couldn't even get past the guard. Years later Landon told a reporter that the humiliating moment spawned a life's decision. "No matter what I did," he said, "I wasn't going to owe anybody a favor. And I didn't expect anything from anybody that had to do with business. . . . I wasn't going to take any garbage from anybody, either."

As it turned out, he didn't have to: A film executive spotted him and suggested that he enroll in Warner Bros. acting school. Soon Landon was performing in TV productions on *Studio One* and *G.E. Theater*. He made his movie debut in 1957 in a cult favorite of the day, *I Was a Teenage Werewolf*—as its werewolf star.

At about the same time, Landon began a stormy marital career. In 1956 he married legal secretary Dodie Fraser, a relationship that lasted six years. He adopted Dodie's son, Mark, and another boy, Josh. The couple divorced in 1962, and in 1963 Landon married model Lynn Noe, with whom he had four children (Michael Jr., Christopher, Leslie and Shawna). He also adopted Noe's daughter, Cheryl. The marriage ended bitterly in 1982. Landon married his third wife, Cindy, a year later. They had two children, Jennifer, now 8, and Sean, 5.

His acting career really took off when he landed the role of Little Joe in *Bonanza*, the first Western series broadcast in color. Landon, Lorne Greene, Dan Blocker and Pernell Roberts made the widowed Cartwright and his boys the first family of the West, and the show enjoyed a 14-year run. Greene took Landon under his wing, but there were clashes on the set with Roberts when Landon began directing episodes. Roberts left the show after six years. (Now *Bonanza*'s last surviving star, Roberts would say nothing more but that he was "deeply grieved by Michael's death.")

Landon's single-minded ferocity began to unfold during the *Bonanza* years. To cope with his emerging fame, he began popping dozens of tranquilizers a day. He eventually kicked the pill habit. "I still work long days," Landon once conceded of his tendency toward overdrive. "I've always had to work very hard in order to be happy."

And work hard he did, before and behind the camera. After he co-developed *Little House on the Prairie* in 1974, Landon began writing episodes. Then with 22 seasons' worth of hit shows as collateral, he brought his idea for *Highway to Heaven* to NBC and, along with *The Cosby Show*, pulled the network out of the ratings cellar. Landon had just completed the pilot for *US*, a series that was to have dealt with family matters, when he became ill.

Four hundred mourners gathered at a Los Angeles memorial service to say goodbye to a talented, stubborn and gallant man who made a wretchedly unhappy childhood the impetus to bring a different sort of reality to television. In an unfinished letter that Cindy found after her husband's death, Landon wrote, "A man's family is everything." □

FRED MACMURRAY

For a dozen years beginning in 1960, Fred MacMurray was pop culture's perfect pop. As the widowed Steve Douglas on TV's *My Three Sons*, MacMurray made fatherhood look enjoyable and rewarding at a time when, to many, the generation gap seemed unbridgeable.

But for all his paternal beneficence, and his well-meant bumbling in Walt Disney comedies like *The Shaggy Dog* (1959) and *The Absent-Minded Professor* (1961), MacMurray the actor was really at his best when he was up to no good. He could show a sinister streak lurking behind the ingratiating grin, and he used it to create the chilling insurance agent who turns to murder with Barbara Stanwyck in *Double Indemnity* (1944), the conniving naval officer in *The Caine Mutiny* (1954) and the philandering executive in 1960's Oscar winner *The Apartment*.

Offscreen, MacMurray was much like his TV persona, an amiable, unaffected husband and father who happened to be a major Hollywood star. Not that his good nature impaired his good business sense. By the time of his death, MacMurray had become one of the richest actors in Hollywood.

By 1943 he was reportedly the highest-paid actor out there, and he invested early and wisely. (Nor did he get rich by squandering his money: MacMurray had a reputation for frugality that would have done Jack Benny proud.)

The only child of a concert violinist, MacMurray was born in Kankakee, Illinois. After his parents separated he was sent to military school, then settled in Wisconsin with his mother. He went to college on a scholarship, taking music courses, then left to study art at the Chicago Art Institute, where he bankrolled himself by playing in a dance band. MacMurray was married twice: to dancer Lillian Lamont, who died in 1953, and to song-and-dance actress June Haver, who came out of a convent to marry him.

MacMurray summed up his career at a 1986 tribute by saying, "Well, I've done pretty good for a guy who plays saxophone." He died of pneumonia at St. John's Hospital and Health Center in Santa Monica. He was 83. □

DANNY THOMAS

In his first TV appearance, on NBC's *All Star Revue*, an early '50s variety show, nightclub headliner and film actor Danny Thomas bombed. He vowed never to return, blasting the medium as "only for idiots." Fortunately for the idiots, Thomas changed his mind (and his act) in 1953 and became one of the youthful medium's most durable stars. Sporting a cigar only slightly longer than his epic nose, mixing verbal sass with moralistic schmaltz, he shaped small-screen humor—along with the likes of buddies Milton Berle and Sid Caesar—for more than four decades. In February, at age 79, he had just appeared on NBC's *Empty Nest* (produced by his son, Tony) and was looking forward to doing a TV movie with daughter Marlo when he was stricken with a fatal heart attack at his Beverly Hills home.

Thomas's *Make Room for Daddy* (later *The Danny Thomas Show*) reigned as a top sitcom from 1953 to 1964, in part because the show's most telling episodes, and even the title, came from the comedi-

Milton Berle, left, and Danny Thomas, 1990.

an's own life. Born Muzyad Yakhoob, the Lebanese-American son of a Toledo dry-goods peddler dropped out of school to follow his star in radio and vaudeville. Like his TV character, he was so often on the road that wife Rose Marie would frequently let one of the children sleep in her bedroom. When Danny came home, they had to make room for Daddy.

More than an actor, he amassed a fortune producing such hits as *The Andy Griffith Show*, *The Dick Van Dyke Show* and *The Mod Squad*. A devout Catholic, Thomas showed his gratitude for success by founding St. Jude Children's Research Hospital in Memphis in 1962. At his memorial service, thronged with two former Presidents—Ford and Reagan—and a pantheon of show business giants that included Berle, Bob Hope, Joey Bishop, Martha Raye, Carl Reiner and Mary Tyler Moore, Thomas's son-in-law, Phil Donahue, eulogized, "We came to think of him as more holy than mortal. This week he proved us wrong. And he broke our hearts." □

Harry Reasoner

HARRY REASONER

It was the twinkle in his eye and the sly, slightly crooked smile that distinguished Harry Reasoner and so endeared him to the American viewing public. In his 35 years as a news correspondent, coanchor on the *ABC Evening News* and especially in his two stints (1968–70, 1978–91) on CBS's celebrated *60 Minutes*, Reasoner traded amiably on a sort of cracker-barrel crankiness that told viewers he was about to let them in on a naughty little secret about important people in high places.

Ironically, as *60 Minutes* evolved into America's favorite muckraking forum, Reasoner often seemed bemusedly out of sync with the show's aggressive style and glitzy tone. In a 1968 essay on boxing and music as escapes from the ghetto, Reasoner dryly observed, "The title of this segment is 'Body and Soul'—and the bright young man who thought that up got the rest of the day off."

Now *60 Minutes* must survive without Reasoner's affable skepticism. After two operations for lung cancer and another to remove a blood clot on his brain, followed by a bout with pneumonia, Reasoner died in a hospital near his Westport, Connecticut, home at age 68. ☐

GEORGE GOBEL

Nobody quite knew why George Gobel was funny, least of all Gobel himself. When his show premiered on NBC in 1954, he tried to explain it to his audience: "Now, it's not the greatest show in the world—I mean it's not hilarious. Jocular is what it—uh, humor . . . well, it might just keep you from getting sullen."

That was Lonesome George, hanging around sheepishly somewhere in the melancholy terrain between Charlie Chaplin and Charlie Brown. Maybe viewers didn't quite get it either, but it didn't stop them from going around parroting Gobelisms like "well-then-there-now" and his permanent self-assessment: "Well, I'll be a dirty bird." His wife figured as the character "Spooky Ol' Alice" in many of his routines. "I've only had one argument with her in all our years together," he told his audience, "but for just two people, we've kept it going pretty good."

His show disappeared after three years, but the comedian kept bobbing up: in movies, in nightclubs and, most notably, as a slow-talking, quick-witted sniper on *Hollywood Squares*. He was 71 when he died in Encino, California. ☐

TENNESSEE ERNIE FORD

helped put country on the map. With a bass-baritone voice the consistency of summer molasses, he took the heartfelt hopes and pentecostal sentiments of the rural South and poured them into the mainstream of American culture. Inducted last year into the Country Music Hall of Fame, Ford died at 72 of complications from a longstanding liver ailment.

Born Ernest Jennings Ford and raised in the small farming community of Bristol, Tennessee, Ernie grew up singing in the local Methodist church. After college, he subsidized his voice studies at the Cincinnati Conservatory of Music with a $10-a-week job as a disc jockey. His nascent singing career was interrupted by World War II, in which Ford served as a bomber-navigator and rose to the rank of lieutenant.

After the war he began singing on Cliffie Stone's *Hometown Jamboree* radio show out of Pasadena, California. Stone persuaded Capitol records to sign Ford in 1948, and he had a string of country hits that crossed over to the pop music charts. And although country types weren't generally considered suitable for television in the early '50s, "the ol' pea picker," as he liked to call himself, made frequent guest appearances, notably as a lovable rube on *I Love Lucy*. In 1953 he became the first country singer to appear at the Palladium in London. But it was the smash success of "Sixteen Tons" that established him as a bona fide star. Written and recorded by his friend Merle Travis in 1947, Ernie's bluesy rendition, which eventually sold more than 20 million copies worldwide, propelled him to his own TV variety show, *The Ford Hour*. Despite an impressive staff of writers—including a young Norman Lear—he frequently rewrote their scripts, inserting such homespun homilies as "Feels like I been rode hard and put away wet" and "Nervous as a long-tailed cat in a roomful of rockin' chairs" into his patter. It worked: The show got top ratings and ran for five seasons. Bless his pea-pickin' heart. ☐

REDD FOXX

It almost seemed as if Redd Foxx, reprising his favorite *mal jeste* from *Sanford and Son*, had clutched his chest and cried once more, "Elizabeth, it's the big one! I'm coming to join you, honey!"—and it happened. It would have suited Foxx's low-down, high-toned sense of drama to orchestrate his own exit in such grand style. After all, this was the man who almost single-handed brought the harsh black comedy of the Chitlin' Circuit into mainstream American culture and cleared the road for such disciples as Richard Pryor and Eddie Murphy.

When Foxx collapsed on Stage 31 of the Paramount lot in Los Angeles, several *Royal Family* cast members assumed it was a gag. Foxx, as was his wont between takes, had been cracking jokes for his colleagues' benefit. Della Reese, who played his TV wife, thought he had taken a pratfall. No one suspected that the 68-year-old comedian, who died of complications from a heart attack, was having any health problems. Coworkers insisted that he was in high spirits, what with a new prime-time TV show and a new wife (his fourth), Korean-born Kaho Cho, 30ish, whom he married last July in Las Vegas.

Born John Elroy Sanford in St. Louis, he started playing with a tramp band on Chicago street corners at age 13. Three years later, in 1938, the group hopped a freight to New York City. There Sanford decided he needed a new name. His friends had called him Fox, for his stylish ways, and Red, because he was carrot-topped. Then he saw the name of the great slugger Jimmie Foxx, and Redd Foxx was born.

He found a place to live on a tenement rooftop with another "Red"—Malcolm Little, later known as Malcolm X, the fiery Black Muslim leader who was gunned down in 1965. (In *The Autobiography of Malcolm X*, Foxx—"Chicago Red"—is described by Malcolm as "the funniest dishwasher on this earth.")

He finally got a stand-up gig in Baltimore. His routines, brutally scatalogical and scathingly funny, began to catch on in black clubs.

After the war he made his way to Los Angeles and began making comedy records. The down-and-dirty Redd Foxx album *Laff of the Party* became a contraband favorite of teens. His albums sold nearly 15 million copies.

By the '60s, Foxx was appearing at Harlem's storied Apollo Theater. The theater's owner, Bobby Schiffman, managed to get a sanitized Foxx on *The Tonight Show*, which in turn led to more TV shots and, finally, an entrée into the gilded rooms of Las Vegas. "I swear to God and any three other white men that you're going to enjoy me," he rasped to middle-class audiences. And they did.

Meanwhile, Hollywood was riding the new wave of black action films; Foxx landed the part of a savvy junkman in 1970's *Cotton Comes to Harlem.* His performance caught the eyes of producers Norman Lear and Bud Yorkin who, on the heels of their success with *All in the Family*, wanted to try a show with black stars about a Los Angeles junkman. Foxx agreed, insisting on two things: using his family name of Sanford and not using hackneyed black dialect. "I don't eat watermelon at home," he said. "I won't on TV."

Sanford and Son ran for six seasons. Nothing in Foxx's later career—or in his private life—quite matched its success. He was a high roller, the kind of profligate spender who never quite had enough left over for the taxman. In 1989 IRS agents entered his three-bedroom Las Vegas home and stripped it clean.

Foxx was excited about getting another shot with *Royal Family*. Said Reese, his pal from their early club days: "He was always speaking about how happy he was. He said he was a man with everything, two new wives and a TV series." □

Redd Foxx

Graham Greene, 1986.

GRAHAM GREENE was
a gentle mad dog of an Englishman who went out in the midday sun in order to give the world a proper talking-to. "I travel because I have to see the scene," the novelist once said. "I can't imagine it." And so Greene set off on a 20th-century pilgrim's progress—Liberia, Mexico, South America, Vietnam—to find the doomed fools, whiskey priests and *pasionarias* of his bleak morality tales. By the time of his death in Switzerland at 86, his 26 novels and sundry works had sold more than 20 million copies and had been translated into 27 languages.

Among his mourners were his estranged wife, Vivien, who at 85 manages a dollhouse museum in Oxfordshire, and Greene's mistress of many years, Yvonne Cloetta, a married Frenchwoman to whom he discreetly dedicated two of his books.

Duplicity and intrigue, love betrayed and motives mixed were the very ingredients of the sort of plots Greene relished throughout his handsomely checkered life. "All writers," he once observed, "have something of the double agent in them." So do English schoolboys whose fathers are the headmaster. Greene *fils* was treated as a spy among the boys at Berkhamsted, where Greene *pére* presided.

At Oxford, Greene flirted with the Communist Party for about three weeks, then embarked on a conventional enough literary career, working as a copy editor at the *Times* of London, then as a film critic, and writing his first novels, including *Orient Express*, *This Gun for Hire* and *Brighton Rock*. When World War II broke out, Greene joined the British secret service, where he met and befriended, among others, Kim Philby, who years later defected to Moscow just before being unmasked as a Soviet mole. (Greene spliced Philby and two codefectors, Guy Burgess and Donald Maclean,

into his 1973 novel, *The Honorary Consul*.)

In Greene's world, political treachery collided with—and often conspired with—feckless religious fervor. Greene had converted to Roman Catholicism before marrying Vivien Dayrell-Browning, an English Catholic, in 1927. They separated in the 1960s after their two children were grown, but Greene maintained an uneasy alliance with the church. As devoutly as Greene sought spiritual truth, he disdained conservative dogma, and he often crossed swords with church hierarchy over his leftist politics. Thus the paradox of Greene: Latin American royalties from his 1982 novel *Monsignor Quixote* reportedly funded Kalashnikov guns for El Salvador's FMLN; Spanish royalties bought prayer books for the Trappist monks of Galicia.

Greene worked on into his 80s in a spare apartment in Antibes high above the Côte d'Azur, writing every morning in longhand with a fountain pen. The product of this labor was a vivid contribution to the literature of dissent, tempered by Greene's doleful view that evil flourishes even when good men do their damnedest. His tales of moral ambiguity eventually lost ground to John le Carré. Yet Le Carré himself looked up to Greene, as did more than a few writers, among them British novelists Muriel Spark and P.D. James. □

DR. SEUSS Even the Grinch
must be blue. Theodore Seuss Geisel, better known as Dr. Seuss —creator of Horton, the elephant who heard a Who, the Cat in the Hat and a difficult-to-classify creature who steadfastly refused Green Eggs and Ham—died at his home in La Jolla, California, after being ill for several months.

The 87-year-old writer and illustrator was the son of a Springfield, Massachusetts, brewer who ran a zoo during Prohibition. Geisel wanted to write serious novels; his first, *Seven Lady Godivas*, published in 1939, was a failure. But his first children's book, *And to Think I Saw It on Mulberry Street*, was a best-seller: Dr. Seuss had found a vocation. Forty-six

Dr. Seuss, c. 1967.

children's volumes followed, selling some 100 million copies. Many of these works contained subtle messages about environmentalism, tolerance and peace. Said old friend Bob Keeshan of *Captain Kangaroo* fame: "He tried to emphasize strong values that not only children but adults need to have in this world." □

RAJIV GANDHI Modern
India's greatest political dynasty may have ended with the assassination at 46 of Rajiv Gandhi in Sriperumpudur, India. Prime Minister from 1984 until 1989, he was killed while campaigning to regain that post. A former airline pilot, Rajiv reluctantly entered politics following the assassination of his mother, Prime Minister Indira Gandhi, in 1984, four years after his politically ambitious brother, Sanjay, had died in a plane crash. Rajiv's maternal grandfather was Jawaharlal Nehru, Prime Minister from 1947 until his death in 1964. Gandhi is survived by his Italian-born wife, Sonia, and their two children. □

Rajiv Gandhi, 1990.

Isaac Bashevis Singer, 1970.

ISAAC BASHEVIS SINGER,
the Nobel-prizewinning author who wrote mystical stories about life in Poland's Jewish shtetls, died at 87 of a stroke in Florida. Raised for the rabbinate in Warsaw, Singer fled from Nazi Europe in 1935 and settled on New York City's Upper West Side, where he recorded the sights and sounds of other immigrants who passed the hours in city parks and pastry shops, haunts that soon became familiar to his readers. Singer, who wrote in Yiddish, published more than 30 novels and short-story collections and saw two of his works, *Yentl* and *Enemies, A Love Story*, become movies. Of the former, which starred Barbra Streisand, he said, "There was too much singing, much too much." □

105

Melvin Franklin, David Ruffin, Otis Williams, Eddie Kendrick, Dennis Edwards, 1989.

DAVID RUFFIN Ah, the Temptations, gliding across the stage in their dazzling mohair suits and spreading the balm of sweet-soul pop over the '60s. Led by David Ruffin's gorgeous, gospel-trained voice, the Temptations carried the Motown banner on up the music charts with hits like "The Way You Do the Things You Do," "Ain't Too Proud to Beg" and, of course, "My Girl," the classic love song of the Big Chill era.

The heart and soul of that music died after arriving in a limousine at a Philadelphia hospital emergency room. The driver reportedly told attendants, "He's in bad shape. He was with the Temptations. His name is David Ruffin," then sped away.

It was indeed Ruffin, 50, who died an hour later. A well-known night prowler, Ruffin had apparently collapsed at a crack house

several hours earlier with up to $40,000 on him—proceeds from a recent European tour. Though the money was missing when he arrived at the hospital, the coroner found no evidence of injury and ruled his death an accidental drug overdose.

Born Davis Eli Ruffin in Meridian, Mississippi, Ruffin moved to Detroit in the late '50s. Changing his name to David, he cut a few unsuccessful singles for Anna Records, owned by a sister of Motown godfather Berry Gordy, and met Temptations cofounder Otis Williams. As the legend goes, David jumped onstage with the group one night and brought down the house by flipping the microphone into the air, spinning, catching it, then collapsing in a split.

That trademark routine would be seen thousands of times after Ruffin joined the Temptations in

1963. With his striking, raspy baritone and Eddie Kendrick's lyrical tenor, the Temps rolled out 16 Top 40 singles in four years before the clash of egos began to unravel the stylish group.

Ruffin left in 1968 to go solo. By then he had already served one stint in a drug-rehabilitation center; a sad string of arrests and failed rehab attempts would follow during the next two decades. Still, in 1989 he and former Temps Kendrick and Dennis Edwards mended fences and resumed touring together. At his death, "He was making money and working steady," said his ex-wife, Sandra, of the father of four. "The only downfall he had was the drugs. He was really trying, but after 24 years with the drugs, he just couldn't conquer it." Even so, she added, "he never lost his voice." □

GEROME RAGNI, who brought the "Age of Aquarius" to Broadway when he cowrote and starred in *Hair*, died of cancer in New York City. Although Ragni later wrote other shows, he was never able to duplicate *Hair*'s success. At the time of his death, he was working with his collaborators from the 1968 smash—writer James Rado and composer Galt McDermot—on a new musical, *Sun*. Ragni was 48. □

CLAUDIO ARRAU, the Chilean-born pianist whose genteel, worshipful renderings of Beethoven and Liszt entranced audiences for 70 years, died at 88 after intestinal surgery in Mürzzuschlag, Austria. □

LARRY KERT, who played the star-crossed Tony in the original 1957 Broadway production of *West Side Story*, died at 60 of AIDS in New York City. □

DOTTIE WEST Even after giving up her home and auctioning her possessions last year to pay off $2.5 million in debts and taxes, country singer Dottie West still talked as tough as the farm girl she'd once been in McMinnville, Tennessee. "I'm a survivor," she proclaimed. "You can knock me down, but you better have a big rock to keep me there."

The 58-year-old singer died tragically in September during surgery at Nashville's Vanderbilt University Medical Center. Five days earlier, the car in which she was riding had gone out of control on a Nashville parkway's elevated exit ramp and crashed nose down onto the roadway below. West had been on her way to perform at the Grand Ole Opry when the accident occurred. She was riding with a neighbor because her own car—a Chrysler New Yorker that singer Kenny Rogers had given her following her money woes last year—had stalled.

West had been one of country music's favorite personalities since the early '60s, when she was among the handful of female songwriters working in Nashville. Her pals included other then-unknowns like Roger Miller and Willie Nelson. She first appeared at the Grand Ole Opry in 1962 and within two years had become the first female country artist to win a Grammy (for her single "Here Comes My Baby"). Over the next two decades, West appeared regularly on the country charts with hits like "Paper Mansions," "A Lesson in Leavin'" and "Country Sunshine," which West had originally written for a Coca-Cola commercial—and which later became her nickname.

Divorced in 1972 from steel-guitar player Bill West, her college sweetheart at Tennessee Tech whom she had married 20 years earlier, Dottie moved on to an eight-year marriage to drummer Byron Metcalf, 12 years her junior. In 1983 she wed her road manager and sound engineer, Alan Winters, who was 22 years younger than she. "I don't feel my age," she explained after her third trip to the altar.

The last two years hadn't been kind to West. She divorced Winters in January 1990 and soon after filed for bankruptcy. Thanks to a debt of more than $1 million, she had most of her possessions—even her stage costumes—confiscated by the government. □

Dottie West, 1989.

Rudolf Serkin at the piano with son Peter, 14, in 1962.

RUDOLF SERKIN, the
avuncular concert pianist whose
dazzling technique kept classical
music audiences rapt for more
than 60 years, died at 88 after a
long illness in Guilford, Vermont.
A native of Austria, Serkin was
more a musician made than a
musician born. Only through sheer
willpower and long hours of practice (he always claimed that he
spent five hours just warming up)
was he able to overcome the hand-
icap of fingers so thick they barely
fit between a piano's black keys.
Serkin is survived by his wife,
Irene, son Peter, also a world-class
pianist, and five other children. □

BILL GRAHAM Brusque,
rumpled and charming to the end,
Bill Graham spent his last hours
the way he loved best—working a
rock show. When the 60-year-old
Graham was killed in a helicopter
crash after leaving the California
concert, the rock world was
stunned.

Graham was known as much
for his charitable fund-raising as
for helping launch the careers of
the Jefferson Airplane, Janis Joplin, the Grateful Dead and other
megastars of the psychedelic '60s.
Three days after the crash—which
killed his companion, Melissa Gold,
as well as pilot Steve Kahn—more
than 2,000 mourners turned out
for Graham's funeral at San Francisco's Temple Emanu-el.

Born Wolfgang Wolodia Grajonca
to Russian Jewish émigrés in Ber-
lin, Graham and Tolla, the youngest of his five sisters, were placed
in an orphanage by their mother
after she was widowed. Sent to
France in an exchange program,
the two remained sheltered there
until Germany invaded in 1940,
and they were forced to flee, on
foot, with 63 other children and a
Red Cross worker. On the way to
Lyon, Tolla died of starvation.
Graham, one of only 11 survivors
of a journey through Europe,
northern Africa and Cuba, arrived
in the U.S. in 1942 and was eventually taken in by foster parents.
When he later learned that his
four sisters had survived the war,
he worked odd jobs to help pay
their passage to the U.S. Drafted
in 1951, Graham was sent to
Korea, where he received a
Bronze Star, a Purple Heart—
and two courts-martial for dis-
obeying orders.

As a promoter in the '60s,
Graham converted an old San
Francisco skating rink into the
Fillmore Auditorium, opened a
sister theater in New York City
and made them the hottest venues
of the era. Backstage with clip-
board and stopwatch one minute,
out front giving patrons free ap-
ples the next, Graham personally
took charge of everything—hiring
the bands, taste-testing the hot
dogs, checking the sound systems
and verbally blistering anyone who
got in his way.

In the 1970s, Graham closed
the Fillmores and began staging
festivals and stadium tours featur-
ing the Rolling Stones, Bob Dylan,
George Harrison and other big-
draw acts. Six years ago he produced the Live Aid benefit concert
in Philadelphia for world famine
relief, characteristically bringing
the 14-hour show to an end only
three minutes over schedule. According to singer Grace Slick,
Graham's great ability was to promote the talents of "a bunch of
hairy, disorganized musicians" who
wouldn't otherwise have made it
in show business. □

DENNIS CROSBY

Bing Crosby's legacy as Daddy Dearest goes on. Two years ago Lindsay Crosby, the youngest of the four sons born to Bing and his first wife, Dixie Lee Crosby, shot and killed himself at 51. His tragedy was reprised in May when his brother Dennis died at 56 in his Novato, California, home, apparently from a self-inflicted shotgun blast.

Friends said Dennis had been increasingly despondent since Lindsay's suicide. Moreover, he had recently broken up with his girlfriend, Meg Muir, and had reportedly begun drinking heavily—though he had been in Alcoholics Anonymous for years.

Dennis, who is survived by a twin brother, Philip, was the quietest of the four boys, though that was no protection against his father's harsh treatment. Though he too suffered the belt whippings amply detailed in eldest brother Gary's 1983 book *Going My Own Way*, Dennis once said, "I let things roll right off me. I don't stay mad long." But an indifferent show business career with his brothers, two broken marriages (he had five children, one illegitimate) and several business failures later, the hurt still lingered. In the end, it was one more refrain in the sad ballad of the boys who could never sing on key for their father. □

From left: Lindsay, Dennis, Bing, Phil and Gary Crosby, 1971.

DAVE GUARD, who

founded the preppy folk group the Kingston Trio in 1957, died at 56 of lymphoma in Rollinsford, New Hampshire. Guard, the banjo-strumming leader, Bob Shane and Nick Reynolds roused fans in the late '50s and early '60s with such hits as "The Ballad of Tom Dooley" and "Scotch and Soda." In 1961, in an unharmonious breakup, Guard left his partners and started a group called the Whiskeyhill Singers. "There were conflicts and bitter feelings," Reynolds said recently. "Dave was the musician. Bob and I just liked to shake our asses and have a good time." □

THE REVEREND JAMES CLEVELAND,

long anointed the King of Gospel, died at 59 of heart failure in Los Angeles. The robust baritone could make church pews shake with his Grammy award-winning songs, including "Peace Be Still," "The Love of God" and "Everything Will Be All Right." In the late 1960s, Cleveland helped spirit gospel out of the choir loft and onto the record charts, acting as collaborator and coach to such performers as Aretha Franklin (who began singing under his tutelage at age 9), Quincy Jones and Edwin Hawkins. □

CLARENCE LEO FENDER died at 82 of un-

known causes in Fullerton, California. The bespectacled tinkerer gave rock and roll its bite when he developed the Stratocaster electric guitar, first introduced in 1954. The Stradivarius of pop, it produced a distinctive, edgy sound that helped define rock's emerging spirit and won him posthumous induction into the Rock and Roll Hall of Fame. The long list of Strat fanciers include Lou Reed, Buddy Holly, Muddy Waters, Keith Richards, Jimi Hendrix and Eric Clapton. □

Stan Getz, 1973.

STAN GETZ, the graceful tenor saxophonist best known for his seemingly effortless "cool jazz," died at 64 of liver cancer in Malibu, California. Getz, who began performing professionally when he was 15, first gained fame in the 1940s and topped the pop charts in 1962 with the bossa nova hit "Desafinado." "When the end comes," said Getz, who waged a lifelong struggle with drugs and alcohol, "the thing that I will be most proud of is that, toward the end of my life, I became what I should have been, a decent gentleman. Or as much of one as I can be, coming from the Bronx." ☐

MILES DAVIS once said that "the history of jazz can be told in four words: Louis Armstrong, Charlie Parker." Make that six. Davis didn't invent jazz; instead, he constantly reinvented it as albums like *Birth of the Cool* (1949), *Kind of Blue* (1959), *Sketches of Spain* (1960) and *Bitches Brew* (1970) lined his restless passage from bebop to cool, modal and jazz-rock fusion. Davis died at 65 of pneumonia, respiratory failure and a stroke in Santa Monica, California.

Renowned for the intensity of his minimalist, achingly sensitive trumpet playing, Davis also flaunted a hip, defiant edge that earned him the sobriquet Prince of Darkness. Brooding and solitary in public, he spurned interviews and seemed to do the same to audiences when he turned his back onstage. Friends say that this was misleading.

"He never did that. He was looking at us," explained Herbie Hancock, one of a legion of famous protégés—including John Coltrane, Cannonball Adderley, John McLaughlin and Keith Jarrett—who learned from master Miles while working in his bands. "He wouldn't focus on the audience, he would focus on the band, on the music." Drum maestro Max Roach, a bandmate from the Charlie Parker days, said Davis "had the musical Midas touch."

Raised in East St. Louis, Illinois,

JIMMY MCPARTLAND & BUD FREEMAN

Two of jazz's luminaries, cornetist Jimmy McPartland and Bud Freeman, a silky tenor saxophonist, put down their instruments for good. McPartland died at 83 of lung cancer in March in Port Washington, New York; Freeman died at 84 of cancer two days later in Chicago. Together they helped create "Chicago jazz," a rough, nervous, driving form of Dixieland that they began playing in the early 1920s as members of Chicago's Austin High [School] Gang, a teenage jazz ensemble that included such legendary clarinetists as Benny Goodman and Frank Teschemacher. In their later, separate careers, McPartland and Freeman played around the world with greats like Louis Armstrong and Gene Krupa. McPartland is survived by his wife, jazz pianist Marian McPartland, 71, whom he married for the second time just two weeks before his death. ☐

CHARLIE BARNET

Saxophonist Charlie Barnet, one of the first white jazzmen to racially integrate his band, died at 77 of pneumonia in San Diego. Barnet, once called "the playboy of the western jazz world," blew an immensely popular brand of swing rooted in the Duke Ellington style and known for its vitality and vigor. He scored his biggest hits in the late '30s and '40s with "Cherokee," "Redskin," "Rhumba" and "Skyliner." "He was one of the good guys," said Lena Horne, who sang with Barnet's band in 1940. "He loved booze, broads, great music and people—no matter what color they were." Barnet was married 11 times. ☐

by his father, a prosperous dentist, and mother, Cleota, an amateur piano player, Miles Dewey Davis III was toying with a trumpet at 10 and studying with his first mentor at 13. By 18, he had already sat in with bebop founders Charlie "Bird" Parker and Dizzy Gillespie when they played St. Louis.

Moving to New York City in 1944, Davis received classical training at the Juilliard School before dropping out to play with Bird and Diz at clubs on 52nd Street. Sharing his apartment and a $40-a-week allowance from home with Parker, he also picked up Bird's worst habit. A heroin addict at 23, Davis went on to supplement his musician's income managing a stable of seven hookers before quitting heroin by 1954.

His body, though, never recovered, in part because he gave it little chance. A chronic insomniac and lifelong chain-smoker, he suffered from sickle-cell anemia, gallstones, cocaine addiction and recurrent complications from a hip injury suffered in a 1969 drive-by shooting. His speaking voice was reduced to a hoarse rasp in 1957 when he permanently damaged his vocal cords in a shouting match with a record executive days after throat surgery to remove polyps. In 1972 he broke both legs in a car accident and by 1975 was bedridden with leg infections, pneumonia and bleeding ulcers. Hooked on codeine and morphine painkillers, he became a recluse in his Manhattan brownstone. For years, he said, "I didn't feel like listening to music. Didn't want to hear it, see it, smell it, nothing about it." In 1981 a hit album, *The Man with the Horn*, revived his career.

Davis credited his relationship with actress Cicely Tyson, his fifth wife, whom he married in 1981, with inspiring his comeback. Davis, who had four children from previous marriages, and Tyson divorced in 1988, and he began spending most of his time at home in Malibu, California. At last summer's Montreux International Jazz Festival, Davis, the artist who never looked back, surprised everyone by sounding a return to his bebop beginnings. □

Miles Davis

PHOTOGRAPHY CREDITS

• Cover, Steve Schapiro • Back Cover, clockwise from top left, Eugene Adebari/Rex USA; James Smeal/ Ron Galella Ltd.; William Campbell/PEOPLE WEEKLY; Tim Graham/ Sygma • Half title page, Chancellor/ Alpha/Globe • Title page, © 1991 Visages • Pages 6-7, William Campbell/PEOPLE WEEKLY

IN THE LIMELIGHT / Page 8, © 1991 Visages • 9, James Smeal/Ron Galella Ltd. • 10, No Credit • 11, Peter C. Borsari • 12, Tristar Pictures • 13, Peter Heimsath/Rex USA • 14, Albert Ortega/Ron Galella Ltd. • 15, Barry King/Gamma Liaison • 16, Dave Lewis/Rex USA • 17, James Smeal/Ron Galella Ltd. • 19, Anthony Barboza • 20, George Lange/ Outline • 21, Dan Borris /Outline • 22, Eugene Adebari/Rex USA • 23, Dana Fineman/Sygma • 24, top to bottom, Joyce Silverstein/Rex USA, Mark Sennet/PEOPLE WEEKLY, Mark Sennet /Onyx • 25, top to bottom, Steve Granitz/ Retna, Terry O'Neill/Sygma

PRIVATE LIVES / Page 26, J. Bourquet/Sygma • 28, Press Association • 29, Nunn Syndication • 30, S. Daniels/ FSP/Gamma Liaison • 31, Tim Graham/ Sygma • 32, top, Darryl Estrine/Onyx, bottom left to right, Wide World, Courtesy of Kris Nelson Tinker • 33, No Credit • 35, Sargent N. Hill

CRIMES & MISDEMEANORS / Page 36, T. Gerson/ L.A. Daily News/Gamma Liaison • 37, left to right, Roger W. Vargo/L.A. Daily News/Gamma Liaison, center (2), Djansezian/AP/Wide World, Diana Walker/Gamma Liaison • 38-39 left to right, Swersey/Gamma Liaison, Jeffrey Markowitz/Sygma • 41, top to bottom, Milwaukee Sentinel/SABA, AP, The Milwaukee Journal/AP • 42, left to right & top to bottom, (4) AP/Wide World, The Milwaukee Journal/Sipa, second row, (3) AP, third row, AP, The Milwaukee Journal/Sipa, AP/Wide World, fourth row, AP/Wide World, The Milwaukee Journal/Sipa, AP/ Wide World • 44, Courtesy of Marilyn Van Derbur Atlar/PEOPLE WEEKLY • 45, UPI/ Bettmann • 46, Christopher Little/Outline • 47, Courtesy of Marilyn Van Derbur Atlar • 49, No Credit • 50, AP/Wide World • 51, AP/Wide World • 53, Evan Richman/ Photoreporters • 54, Carlos Rios/The Houston Chronicle • 55, No Credit • 56, UPI /Bettmann • 57, No Credit • 58, ABC • 59, Wilbur Fuches /Gannet Westchester Papers • 60-61, Kimberly Butler/ PEOPLE WEEKLY • 62, No Credit • 63, left to right, No Credit, Scott Weiner/Retna

PROVOCATIONS / Page 64-65 left to right, Lee Celano/ UPI/Bettmann, L.D. Ligier/Ron Galella Ltd., Remy LeMorvan/Bettmann • 66, Justin Thomas/ Retna • 67, Steve Allen/Gamma Liaison • 68, Peter C. Borsari • 69, top to bottom, Mark Sennet/Onyx, ABC

PROFILES IN COURAGE / Page 70, Christopher Little/Outline • 72-73, Henry Grossman • 75, D. Gordon/ Onyx • 76-77, AP/Wide World • 78-79, Esais Baitel/ Gamma Liaison • 79, Steve Hirsch/Globe • 80, Harry Benson • 81, Dennis Brock/Black Star • 82, Andy Freeberg/PEOPLE WEEKLY • 83, Dominique Aubert/Sygma • 84-85, Terry Ashe/Time Magazine

POSTSCRIPTS / Page 87, left to right, Photofest, Phil Roach/Photoreporters • 88, left, Don Ornitz/ Globe Photos, right, (2) Tony Costa/Outline • 89, left, John Olson/LIFE Magazine, right, No credit • 90, top, Mark Sennet, center, John Barrett/Globe, bottom, left to right, Darryl Estrine/ Onyx, Robert Landau/ Globe Photos • 91, top, right to left, Globe Photos, Susan Aimee Weinik/PEOPLE WEEKLY, bottom, left to right, Tony Costa/Outline, No Credit

GOODBYES / Page 92, Steve Schapiro/Gamma Liaison • 93, Dwight Whitney • 94, Photofest • 95, top left, Lester Glassner Collection/Neal Peters, top right, AP/Wide World, bottom, No Credit • 96, Rob Brown/Onyx • 97, Gjon Mili/ LIFE Magazine • 98, UPI/Bettmann • 99, UPI/Bettmann • 100, Photofest • 101, James Smeal/Ron Galella Ltd. • 102, Ken Regan/ Camera 5 • 103, Gail Harvey/Outline • 104, top to bottom, UPI/Bettmann, Helen Miljakovich • 105 (2) UPI/Bettmann • 106, Robin Platzer/ Images • 107, AP/Wide World • 108, UPI/Bettmann • 109, UPI/ Bettmann • 110, The Collection of Neal Peters • 111, Chuck Pulin/Star File